THE GREEN BERET
SURVIVAL GUIDE

THE GREEN BERET SURVIVAL GUIDE

ADVICE ON SITUATIONAL AWARENESS, PERSONAL SAFETY, RECOGNIZING THREATS, AND AVOIDING TERROR AND CRIME

BRIAN M. MORRIS

MASTER SERGEANT (RETIRED),
UNITED STATES ARMY SPECIAL FORCES

Skyhorse Publishing

Skyhorse Publishing books may be purchased in bulk at special discounts for sales promotion, corporate gifts, fund-raising, or educational purposes. Special editions can also be created to specifications. For details, contact the Special Sales Department, Skyhorse Publishing, 307 West 36th Street, 11th Floor, New York, NY 10018 or info@skyhorsepublishing.com.

Skyhorse® and Skyhorse Publishing® are registered trademarks of Skyhorse Publishing, Inc.®, a Delaware corporation.

Visit our website at www.skyhorsepublishing.com.

10 9 8 7 6 5 4 3 2 1

Library of Congress Cataloging-in-Publication Data is available on file.

Cover design by Brian Peterson
All photos copyright the author unless otherwise noted.

Print ISBN: 978-1-5107-4075-4
Ebook ISBN: 978-1-5107-4076-1

Printed in China

Dedication

I dedicate this book to my superhero wife AnnMarie, who kept by my side through an arduous military career, almost singlehandedly raised our children, nursed me back to health from the death grip of cancer, and comforted me on many a restless night when the blood-stained sands of war came to visit me in my sleep;
I will always love you, angel.

Table of Contents

APPENDICES

Foreword

Cork Graham, *New York Times* best-selling author of *The Bamboo Chest*

One thing is certain and that is that the age of innocence is long gone for the United States. Things that we once took for granted are now very close to the forefront of our everyday thoughts and actions. Remember when going on an airline flight was like going to the opera or walking down the red carpet? Travel and airline travel were momentous events. Long before I was born, people boarded trains and ships, elegantly dressed, with an entourage, traveling with months of clothes and other belongings—not in small suitcases designed for overheads, with wheels that seem to pop off at the most inopportune time, but in full-sized chests made of wood and brass, made to last. When you boarded a plane in the pre-1970s, you *were* a movie star.

Then in 1968, the longest commercial hijacking for political purposes occurred, and the rest of the early 1970s was rife with these types of hijackings, so much so that major changes were made at airports. When you could once take hunting rifles and even handguns as personal carry-ons, firearms were now stowed in check-in luggage, and metal detectors and x-ray machines were installed at airport gates. Suddenly travel changed. So shocking then, these procedures are taken as normal operating procedures nowadays.

Travel took on a whole new quality that made many feel as if they were now navigating a world of threats and suspicions and violent people. Mind you, those types of people—those types of predators—were always there. They will always be there. The question is what will you do to prepare yourself to understand the world in which we live, one that requires a level of awareness and willingness to do what must be done and that many, frankly, are not willing to do. This is stupid and naïve in my view, as I'm sure it is in the mind of Brian Morris, who has written an excellent guide to getting yourself squared away to face the many possible threats that can occur while traveling these days.

The gravity of having this understanding, this willingness to do what is necessary, and consequences of not doing so should not be taken lightly—all it takes is one incident of bodily harm to change or end your life.

Of course, all opinions are based subjectively on the thinker's formative environment. Many of us were brought up in a First World type of lifestyle, where we were offered the luxury of always having essential needs such as food, water, and shelter. This is not the case in so many locations around the world. Having worked in some real hell-holes, I'm sure Brian and I share mutual understandings that, given the opportunity to be good, people will be so. Those aren't the ones to be prepared for, other than to make sure their good nature is never ignored.

Sadly, in the places that President Trump once called "shit-holes," people aren't often given that luxury, and will fight tooth and nail for anything of worth in their part of the world—and it breeds a very cynical and angry type of individual. Years in war zones have taught me that patriotic rhetoric is fine, but what really starts a populace picking up weapons and fighting uprisings is hunger. It's for this very reason that "bread and circuses," or these days, "free cell phones and food stamps" has been so successful in placating a populace that only two hundred years earlier was willing to fight a revolution over a few words: "taxation without representation."

Every once in a while, an environment creates a type of individual who will go further than a pickpocketing, or robbery, and falls into the classification of flat-out predatory psychopathic behavior.

These types get pleasure from control, creating fear in others, and doing so by kidnapping and murder. Ted Bundy and John Wayne Gacy come immediately to mind, though there are so many more wicked and evil individuals over the centuries who might not have received the same amount of press, but outshine the former in their depravity. It's these kinds of individuals that teach us all that preparedness and being alert is not about being paranoid, that there are real monsters out there who are so willing to take someone out, if for just the sick and twisted pleasure of making someone suffer a tortured and horrific death.

It's these types, but also the various pickpockets, flim-flam men, and even natural disasters that make Brian Morris's new book, *The Green Beret Survival Guide*, timely and important. Within these pages you'll see how an operator thinks and strategizes, and how you, with tactics for a variety of scenarios that include emergency response, dealing with crime, and knowing which rooms in a hotel are best for the safety of you and your loved ones, can counter them.

There are many books about thinking and planning like an operator sent to a foreign country to fight a variety of wars, but how practical is that information for the common man and woman, who are simply driving to another state to see a relative, or getting on a plane to attend a conference? What Brian Morris has done is take some very high level understandings of traveling while on certain kinds of deployments he would have gone on as a combat veteran of the US Army's Special Forces, and taken not only that training, but also the real life experience, and boiled it all down into palatable information bites that will educate and prepare the reader for just about any threat that the average reader could encounter.

I commend you on your book purchase, and I wish you a great experience learning information that anyone wanting to improve the security in their lives will gladly absorb.

—Cork Graham
Bestselling author of *The Bamboo Chest*, and former team
leader on the Discovery Channel's 2015 hit series,
Treasure Quest: Snake Island.

Introduction

After more than seventeen years of war, the United States and its citizens remain vulnerable to a terrorist attack by a ruthless enemy intent on instilling fear and doubt into the hearts and minds of Americans both at home and abroad. Even without the possibility of terrorism, it is a dangerous world filled with criminals and thieves who have the potential to take our property or do us harm. It is imperative that Americans remain vigilant while still conducting their usual business and living their lives fully, either at home in the United States or while traveling abroad. Risk exists and can never be fully eradicated. However, by following the guidelines in this book, it is my honest hope that you may learn to recognize and mitigate the risks that do exist and to make yourself and your loved ones far safer in the process.

The warrior fights with his mind, body, and soul. Photo credit: GettyImages

1

Situational Awareness, the Warrior Mindset, and the Psychology of Survival

SITUATIONAL AWARENESS

The first and most important step to learning the warrior mindset is to develop your situational awareness. Situational awareness is nothing more than staying alert, being aware of your surroundings, and understanding the reality of threats that you may face in any given situation. An individual with good situational awareness practices mindfulness to help them to better understand the fluid

Afghan children chasing our patrol. We usually knew we were not going to make enemy contact when we rolled through a village and there were children out playing.

It never ceased to amaze me how quickly children grow up in a war zone. This Afghan child of maybe six is leading a camel filled with supplies back to his village by himself with no adult supervision.

and ever-changing environment around them. It is this awareness which allows them to increase or decrease their level of vigilance accordingly and to remain grounded and ready to face any challenge with calmness and confidence.

THE WARRIOR MINDSET

The path to becoming a warrior is not an easy one. At its core is discipline. A warrior is a master of spherical awareness, he is ever vigilant, he keeps his head on a swivel, knows his operational environment, can improvise, adapt, and overcome all adversities, and while he is able to accept that he is not invincible, he never runs from adversity, but instead faces it head on. The warrior fights with his mind, body, and soul, and while he has emotions, he must master keeping them at bay in order to fight without letting them interfere with his clarity and lucidity. None of these things will come easily, so do not be discouraged. The only path to mastering anything, particularly the warrior arts, is through hard work and due diligence. Now it is particularly difficult to master anything in the physical world until you conquer your own demons, such things in your head as fear, anxiety, panic, and self-doubt. Once you are able to eliminate these debilitating and useless thoughts, you can move forward in mastering the warrior mindset.

FEAR, ANXIETY, AND PANIC

A warrior must control his fear and anxiety in order to diminish

The root of fear, anxiety, panic, and self-doubt is lack of experience. Photo Credit: GettyImages

panic and maintain clarity while projecting self-confidence toward the eyes of his enemy.

The root of fear, anxiety, panic, and self-doubt is lack of experience. Having a warrior mind-set means being able to set aside or subdue your fear and anxiety so as not to panic in the face of danger, and to diminish self-doubt and project self-confidence toward the eyes of any opponent. Confucius once said, "He who conquers himself is the mightiest warrior."

STRESS INOCULATION

Once you learn to subdue your fear and vanquish panic, you will be on your way to achieving the warrior mindset. The biggest contributor to fear and panic is the unknown. The best way to conquer the unknown is to not only face it, but dive head first into it. By engulfing yourself in your fear, you will achieve "stress inoculation," where you will be able to function and think with clarity even under conditions where your response would previously have been to panic.

An example of the stress inoculation technique would be something I went through personally. I am and always have been deathly

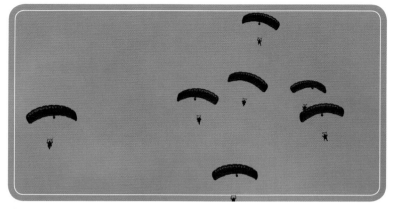

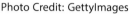
Photo Credit: GettyImages

afraid of heights. That said, in my twenty-five years in the Army, first as a soldier, then as a paratrooper, and then becoming and serving as a Green Beret, I have had to do many things from great heights. This includes maneuvering over high (and unforgiving) obstacles, climbing fifty-foot-high ropes, rappelling off of one-hundred-foot towers, soaring above the trees under a fast-moving chopper in a Spies (Special Patrol Insertion/Extraction System) rig after a jungle extraction, F.R.I.E.S. (Fast Rope Insertion/Extraction System) roping out of helicopters hovering ninety feet above the ground, static line parachuting onto drop zones around the globe with full combat equipment from eight-hundred feet, and jumping from an airplane

from 25,000 feet with an oxygen tank, eighty pounds of equipment, a ram-air parachute on my back, and my weapon strapped to my side, into the dark of night. I was able to do all of these things, not because I am

The author (left) descends down from a HAHO (High Altitude High Opening) jump of over 20,000 feet (circa 2000).

Special Operations Forces (SOF) use S.P.I.E.S (Special Patrol Insertion Extraction System) to rapidly insert and or extract small recon patrols and sniper teams from areas where a helicopter can't land.

particularly courageous, but simply because I had the discipline to face and inoculate myself with my own fears so that I could, if not vanquish my fears completely, at least hold them at bay to a point where I could do my job with clarity of mind and with the absence of panic.

The author's Special Forces unit on patrol in the mountains of northeastern Afghanistan, along the volatile Afghan Pakistan border (circa 2008).

FACING FEAR

A warrior never runs from adversity. Being a warrior is about showing up to the fight when every bone in your body tells you to run in the opposite direction. It's about striving for greatness so that you

Being a warrior is about showing up to the fight when every bone in your body tells you to run in the opposite direction. Photo Credit: GettyImages

know either the elation of high achievement and victory or the pain of defeat. In any case, you can hold up your head proud knowing that you showed up to the fight as opposed to running and hiding, as is the choice of so many of the timid masses.

CITIZENSHIP IN A REPUBLIC SPEECH
BY THEODORE ROOSEVELT

Theodore Roosevelt said in his 1909 Citizenship in a Republic speech that:

> "It is not the critic who counts; not the man who points out how the strong man stumbles, or where the doer of deeds could have done them better. The credit belongs to the man who is actually in the arena, whose face is marred by dust and sweat and blood; who strives valiantly; who errs, and comes short again and again, because there is no effort without error and shortcoming; but who does actually strive to do

the deeds; who knows the great enthusiasms, the great devotions; who spends himself in a worthy cause; who at the best knows in the end the triumph of high achievement, and who at the worst, if he fails, at least fails while daring greatly, so that his place shall never be with those cold and timid souls who know neither victory nor defeat."

Theodore Roosevelt was a true warrior statesman. Photo Credit: GettyImages

OVERRIDING YOUR FEARS

What defines you as a true warrior is your ability to face adversity, and that doesn't mean you have to be a hero or that you're some

You have to have the mentality that you're going to put yourself into the fight no matter what the situation is, particularly if you have brothers who are in the fight. You have to get in there and to help them against any odds. Photo Credit: GettyImages

kind of a superman, because I can tell you from personal experience that one of the most difficult things in the world is to override the basic human instinct to protect yourself. As a warrior there will be times where you may have to have the discipline to counter your innate human instinct to remain safe and to then run toward the sound of enemy gunfire. It's having the mentality that you're going to put yourself into the fight no matter what the situation is, particularly if you have brothers who are in the fight, to get in there and to help them against any odds.

GOOD FORM AND REPETITION ARE THE KEYS TO SUCCESS

Any time you look at people who are successful at doing something, you will find that they usually got that way by learning the proper way of doing something, and then applying due diligence, repeating that same skill over and over again until it became second nature. One of the other traits of successful people is that they are able to learn from other people's mistakes. They can also look at other people who are successful and break down, in a simple way, why they were successful. Then they apply that to their own life.

If you've practiced bad technique over and over again, then you've gotten really good at doing something really badly. Photo Credit: GettyImages

I try to do that as much as possible. When it's something that I don't know about, I look for somebody who is good at it and I see how they do it, then I try to basically mimic what they are doing. The one thing that I have always tried to do is stay good at a few skills. The way to do that is to pick out the skills that are, in your mind, the most important skills to maintain and then make practicing those skills an integral part of your day, just like brushing your teeth or reading the paper.

The way to master a skill is through repetition; just doing that task over and over again with really good technique. Learn how to do it the right way, as technique is everything. If you've practiced bad technique over and over again, then you've gotten really good at doing something really badly. It's important to get the correct technique down in whatever it is that you're trying to learn, be it fighting, yoga, or finger painting. Try to remember that all skills are perishable, and just because you are the master of a skill today does not guarantee that you will be a master five years from now if you don't continue to practice. If you really want to maintain those skills, then the only way to do it is through practice and through making it a part of your everyday life.

BE FLEXIBLE

A warrior is flexible, and knows how to improvise, adapt, and overcome. It's important to remember that techniques sometimes need to change when situations change, and it is up to you to learn or relearn what you need to know in order to maintain mastery of your chosen discipline. For instance, when I was in the Special Forces it was imperative that I be highly proficient at transitioning from my rifle to my pistol as rapidly as possible if my rifle ran out of bullets or malfunctioned. Well, I am retired from the military now and it is no longer a necessity for me to be able to quickly transition from rifle to pistol, as I no longer carry a rifle as part of my everyday carry. I do, however, always carry a concealed pistol. The physical act of drawing a concealed pistol from a concealed pistol holster happens to be much different from drawing a pistol out of a leg holster, so it was back to the drawing board for me. I had to completely change my technique and basically relearn what I was doing in order to become as proficient and lethal at drawing my pistol from a concealed holster as I was when I was in the military and I drew from a tactical leg holster. So remember, you can't just live off the fact that you knew how to do something a long time ago and expect that those skills are going to stay with you for life. You have to maintain and in some cases modify those as you go along, If nothing else, you should continue to practice, no matter how good you think you are at any given discipline.

A WARRIOR WILL NEVER QUIT!

The Spartans said that "any army may win while it still has its legs under it; the real test comes when all strength is fled and the men must produce victory on will alone."

Having the will to fight on and not to quit on yourself is more of a trait than it is something you can learn through conditioning. A warrior's heart is not afraid of death so much as it fears a life lived without honor, loyalty, and standing up for what is right. A warrior never leaves a fallen comrade behind and only needs to look to his left and right to find a reason not to quit but to keep the will to drive on until the war is won!

THE PSYCHOLOGY OF SURVIVAL: CONTROLLING YOUR EMOTIONS AND THINKING ON YOUR FEET

Life is not an action movie. Actors use the magic of Hollywood to make them seem invincible but the reality is that in the real world there are no stunt coordinators, bats and clubs are not

Personal courage, emotional connection, training, and motivation are all factors that can override fear in times of danger where lives depend on your ability to maintain your composure and get the job done. Photo Credit: GettyImages

cardboard, rocks are not paper machete, and guns shoot real bullets. In a real, potentially dangerous or life-threatening situation, running away is not always a bad option. If you sense danger and your mind tells you to run, then either you are not trained and conditioned to react to that particular situation or the threat is just so overwhelming that it is beyond anything that your subconscious thinks you are prepared to deal with. This is not to say that you should not stand and fight if you are ready and able to do so. I have personally been in situations where I had to run as fast as I could toward the sound of (enemy) automatic gun fire in order to support my comrades in need on the battlefield. The hard part is to over-ride common sense in order to intentionally put yourself in harms way. Personal courage, emotional connection, training, and motivation are all factors that can override the freeze and flight parts of the response and propel you forward to engage the danger, whatever it may be.

THE ACUTE STRESS RESPONSE

The acute stress response—also known as the fight, flight, or freeze response—is hardwired into the human psyche. This is how our ancient ancestors were able to act appropriately when facing a

The acute stress response is hardwired into the human psyche as a result of millions of years of evolution. Photo Credit: GettyImages

dangerous animal or when fighting an enemy. In the moment of danger, the blood on the surface of your skin reduces so that the blood flow can increase in your arms, legs, shoulders, eyes, brain, ears, and nose. This physiological change increases all of your senses, making you extremely alert, and it transfers the blood flow to your arms and legs so you can fight or run. While fighting and fleeing are possible choices you can make, freezing, or simply doing nothing is, while not always a good choice, still an option.

FIGHT, FLIGHT, FREEZE

These are some other physiological and psychological signs of the fight, flight, freeze response that human beings may experience when they are faced with a threat:

FIGHT

- Trembling out of anger
- Increased heart rate
- Hands in fists, desire to punch, rip
- Flexed/tight jaw, grinding teeth, snarl
- Fight in eyes, glaring, fight in voice
- Desire to stomp, kick, smash with legs, feet
- Feelings of anger/rage
- Knotted stomach/nausea, burning stomach
- Feeling like a volcano is erupting inside of you
- Bursts of above average strength compared to normal ability

FLIGHT/FREEZE:

- Trembling legs
- Holding breath/shallow breathing
- Screams of fear
- Terrified look on face
- Sweating profusely
- Loss of use of small muscle groups
- Able to quickly move out of the way or run away

THE PHYSIOLOGY OF STRESS

In today's modern world of precision weaponry, fighters are often required to maintain steady breathing and body position and make slow, calculated movements while under extremely stressful and dangerous situations. Photo Credit: GettyImages

Humans are uniquely designed with all the physical potentials and psychological instincts needed to either club a wild boar on the head, thrust a pointed stick into a woolly mammoth, run up a tree to escape being eaten by a saber-toothed tiger, or outrun a tribe of Neanderthals trying to crush your skull with rocks. That said, in today's modern world of precision weaponry, fighters are often required to maintain steady breathing and body position and make slow, calculated movements requiring the use of small motor skills.

The problem is that along with these feelings and displays of behavior comes a loss of fine motor skills needed to react quickly and lethally in response to the threat in order to give you a tactical advantage. The fight, flight, freeze response can also result in a surge of adrenaline that can result in tremors that can affect your stability, surefootedness, and accuracy needed to neutralize any threat or threats you may come up against. Finally, the natural fight, flight, freeze response can result in a severe decrease in spherical awareness as the mind becomes fixated on the perceived threat is if in tunnel vision.

HOW TO TURN ANIMAL INSTINCT INTO A MODERN PRECISION THREAT RESPONSE

I always say, "Never get in a foxhole with someone braver than you are." Photo Credit: GettyImages

The threats today are no less real than they were to our ancient ancestors. How is it that we can control our physiological and psychological responses to danger in such a way as to be able to overcome some of these natural reactions to danger and perform the actions necessary to eliminate the threats that we are faced with?

The answer is stress inoculation coupled with repetitive training techniques. This allows us to turn specific motor skills into natural bodily movements that require little to no conscious thought. In the Special Forces we called it "muscle memory." Now obviously muscles do not have actual memories, but by engraving a specific motor task into your memory by way of repetition, you will eventually gain the ability to perform that task without any conscious effort.

Think of what happens when a child runs out into the road up in front of your vehicle while you are driving. You immediately take your right foot off the gas pedal and place it on the brake pedal. Unless you are brand new to driving, chances are that this action required very little thought. By using repetitive training techniques it is possible to achieve this same level of muscle memory, or Zen, in any of the lethal arts. When I first began learning the Special Forces way of fighting, I started by simply learning to draw my pistol. It was almost two months before I actually fired a live round. I wore my rig, consisting of a pistol belt, spare mag pouch, and a leg "drop" holster that was attached to my pistol belt and strapped to my leg. I had my F92 Berretta 9mm service pistol with a magazine of dummy rounds and I spent hour upon hour and day upon day practicing drawing my pistol from the holstered and secured position, running it up my side, then joining my firing hand to my non-firing hand at my sternum. I then picked up a sight picture on a target and fully extended my arms either into a completely extended fighting stance or placed my finger on the trigger and simultaneously extended my hands and pulled the trigger so that the hammer would fall at the exact moment when my arms were fully extended. I would then put the weapon on safe and then back onto fire in order to de-cock the pistol, and I would re-holster the gun and start the process all over again. I'm not sure how many thousands of times they would make us do these drills but I can tell you that they helped to build a muscle memory foundation that I would have for the rest of my life. Now this was of course just the foundation of our training. After advanced rifle and pistol training, we would learn to use a whole arsenal of other weapons from sniper weapon systems, recoil-less rifles, mortars, and even Naval gun fire, to learning how to fight with a knife or simply with our bare hands. The Green Berets pride themselves on being able to conduct precision operations where threats are neutralized with surgical precision and collateral damage is minimal to nonexistent. This requires each member of the team to be trained to perform their duties flawlessly under enormous amounts of stress in the most arduous environments. The only way to do this is to first train in your individual tasks until you are at a point of muscle memory and then train with your other team members to not only complete your own tasks to perfection, but also to be able to step in and complete the tasks of any of the other members of the team if needed. To accomplish this elite level of training, it is imperative that you ensure that the conditions are stressful enough so that you will eventually become inoculated to the stress and physiological changes that take place when we face danger. They will be kept at bay to a point where we can still function and accomplish our mission. It is good to have a little bit of fear when you are doing dangerous operations. The fear will help you by making you hyper alert to any potential threats and can be quite beneficial in a combat-like scenario. I always say, "Never get in a foxhole with someone braver than you are."

TRAINING AND PREPARATION: THERE IS NO SUBSTITUTE FOR DUE DILIGENCE AND HARD WORK

Photo Credit: GettyImages

So, obviously it is not realistic to expect to be able to train yourself to the elite level of our Special Operations Forces. That kind of training costs millions of dollars and requires a specific type of person who must be disciplined and committed enough to spend years of time solely dedicated to training in order to achieve the level of mindfulness required to override the body's natural response to run or freeze when faced with overwhelming danger and extremely high risk of loss of life. They are able to do this successfully through

If you want to be excellent at something, you need to learn excellent technique and then practice until perfect. There is no shortcut to obtaining experience. If you truly want to improve, then you must be willing to dedicate yourself to hard work and laser focus.

intense and prolonged training and rehearsals coupled with every man on the team taking part in the extremely detailed planning process. The fact that each man knows every plan intimately and has rehearsed and trained to ad nauseam on standard operating procedures and contingency plans for when things don't go as planned is what allows these elite fighters to mitigate risks from a suicidal level down to an acceptable level of risk.

The good news is that you don't have to train like a Green Beret or a Navy SEAL to prepare yourself to override your natural desire to run from a threat. A good example of how to do this kind of training is something I experienced back in my beginning years as a Green Beret on Fort Bragg, North Carolina. Special Forces soldiers and Special Operators in general normally practice some form of mixed martial arts or what the Army calls "Combatives Training." We did this on a regular basis in order to prepare for those contingencies where you either can't get to your weapon fast enough to neutralize a threat, you run out of ammunition, or you simply need to take out an adversary without bringing unwanted attention to yourself. At this time in my career my ODA (Special Forces Operational Detachment-Alpha) was training under Master Ronald Don Vito, a retired Marine Master Gunnery Sergeant who was the senior trainer at one point for the USMC's hand-to-hand combat program and who was the founder of the L.I.N.E system of fighting. L.I.N.E stands for *Linear Infighting Neural Override Engagement.* In short, it is a fighting style that requires you to be able to execute all of the techniques effectively and with proper form while under low-light conditions or other impaired visibility conditions (i.e., smoke or gas), under extreme mental and physical fatigue, and while wearing full combat gear. Ron had a highly effective (some might call it sadistic) way of testing each of us at the end of each day of training called the "swarm." To execute the swarm, the student being tested would have to get into full "battle rattle" or full kit, meaning that you had all of your body armor and equipment on that you would normally be wearing when outside of the wire in a combat environment. Sometimes we would do this in low-light conditions or he would add some smoke to lower visibility when we were training outdoors. Once kitted up, the rest of the students would, on Ron's order, commence to kicking your ass using L.I.N.E techniques, and your only defense was to use the L.I.N.E counter-moves to defend yourself and strike back. And if you are thinking you would just run, forget about it because the other students had orders to chase after you to the parking lot, the woods . . . wherever the fight took them! I can remember a similar Don Vito training method when we were learning to fight with knives where Ron would make us use stun guns in place of harmless rubber training knives that would deliver a high voltage and low current sting every time you touched your sparring partner with it. Well, I can tell you that these are both examples of ways to maximize your ability to train under stressful conditions, while remaining in a controlled environment with safety precautions in place and all without breaking the bank!

Like I said earlier, you don't have be a Navy SEAL or a Green Beret to train realistically and effectively; you simply need to think outside the box in order to create an environment that will allow you to practice under enough stress to allow you to focus and execute under duress, building skill, confidence, and ultimately making you better at whatever it is you are trying to learn to do. No matter if it is shooting, mixed martial arts, or any of the lethal arts, if you are willing to put in the time, energy, and dedication, you can train yourself to a level where you can confidently and effectively stand and fight or get up and run toward the sound of bullets when duty or obligation calls.

Stay calm. The first thing that is going to kick in i[s]
your fight or flight reflex, and your adrenaline is
going to be flowing. You need to be aware of thi[s]
and try to continue to breathe and maintain you[r]
calmness and your situational awareness.

2

Self Defense, Personal Security, and Active Shooter Defense

HOW TO DEFEND YOURSELF IN AN ASSAULT

Not everyone is trained to defend themselves, and reading this book is not going to prepare you to deal with a physical confrontation. The ability to fight off an assailant comes from training your body through muscle memory over a long period of time.

While this is not a book on weapons training or marksmanship skills, I do highly suggest that anyone who is capable and willing to do so should invest the time and effort into learning how to defend yourself with a firearm. I also suggest that you get a concealed carry permit if you can or, if it is permissible, that you carry openly. Choosing not to have constant access to a firearm, and not having the training and confidence to use it to defend yourself and your loved ones, is simply irresponsible in this day and age.

Like much of the information in this book, the answer is in preparation. Self-defense, be it martial arts, firearms training, or any other training that will give you an advantage in a fight, is highly recommended for anyone interested in self-preservation or being able to defend their loved ones if it becomes necessary. You should begin to prepare yourself now for such a contingency by seeking out this training and dedicating yourself to learning how to defend yourself. That said, if attacked, or if you sense that you are about to be attacked, there are a few things you can do to shift the advantage in your favor:

CONTROL YOUR EMOTIONS

Stay calm. The first thing that is going to kick in is your fight or flight reflex, and your adrenaline is going to be flowing. You need to be aware of this and try to continue to breathe and maintain your calmness and your situational awareness.

TRAIN TO BECOME A MASTER MARKSMAN

Photo Credit: GettyImages

If you have a pistol, it is imperative that you train to access it in an emergency as quickly and smoothly as possible and then be prepared to dispense it effectively in a split second. The only way to get to this level of proficiency is through due diligence of repetition coupled with good form. The time to start training to use your weapon in a crisis is not when it is happening, so be sure to be proficient with your firearm if you are planning on having it with you. All of that said, if you feel an assault is imminent, then that would be the time to employ your weapon in order to protect either yourself or others around you.

WHEN DEFENDING YOURSELF WITH A FIREARM IS NOT AN OPTION

Photo Credit: GettyImages

You may not be able to have a firearm on you at all times, but that doesn't mean there are not weapons around you wherever you go. All it takes is some imagination. It honestly doesn't really matter what it is: A Ronald McDonald trophy cracked over an assailant's skull will put him down as quickly as any steel baseball bat. The idea is to simply try to always have something in your hand to temporarily incapacitate an assailant if your senses tell you that you're in bad guy territory. It can be something as sophisticated as a stun gun or mace, or something as basic as a hot cup of coffee or tea that you can throw in a would-be assailant's face before making your escape or fighting through the situation.

If you are not prepared to fight, don't, unless you have no other choice. Even if you are prepared to fight, do not fight unless you absolutely have to. If the opportunity is there for you to throw something at the assailant and run, then do it. Don't be too proud to scream out for help if there are other people in the area.

Always pay specific attention to your assailant's hands; that is most likely where the threat is going to come from. No one has ever been killed by a stare or facial expression.

Once the decision to fight has been made, do not commit half-heartedly. You must commit 100 percent. Violence of action is the key to ending a fight quickly and opening up an opportunity for you to escape. Pay particular attention to the most sensitive parts of your assailant's body, such as eyes, ears, nose, throat, groin, and solar plexus.

You can gouge your thumbs into your attacker's eyes and blind them, or slam your open palms with all your force against your attacker's ears, as this will disorient him momentarily.

In a life-and-death situation, you can take your hand open palmed and slam it into your assailant's nose in an upward direction or use the knife-edge of your hand to slam into your attacker's windpipe.

If your assailant is a man, you can either kick him in the groin, or grab, twist, and pull his groin to momentarily slow him down and give yourself a chance to escape.

You can kick, punch, or elbow your attacker in the solar plexus to knock the wind out of him and give yourself a chance to escape.

Palm to Chin: A variation of the palm-to-nose is the heel of your hand to the lower chin of your assailant. Slam the heel of your palm under your assailant's chin in an upward motion. This may deter your attacker long enough for you to get away.

Eye Gouge: When attempting an eye gouge technique, insert your thumbs into the inside of your assailant's eye sockets and work your way out.

Improvised Weapon Idea: A magazine is an inconspicuous thing to carry around with you. When rolled tightly, a magazine makes a formidable improvised weapon. Use it like a baton by holding it in the center and stabbing in either backward or forward thrusts. Another idea is to carry a glass soda bottle (very prevalent in third world countries). If you have to use it as a weapon, don't break the bottom off on the ground like you see in the movies, as this will probably only destroy the bottle and cut your hand. Instead, hold it at the neck and use the bottom end of the bottle like a club.

In an absolute worst-case scenario where you can't escape and are not able to defend yourself, you must protect your most vulnerable parts: your head and your internal organs. Do this by going into the fetal position and using your arms and hands to protect your head.

The second you have a chance to escape, do it. Seek medical attention immediately if needed. Remember to report the incident to the police or the embassy immediately.

Remember, in a survival situation there is no such thing as a fair fight. Find a weapon. It can be anything: keys, a stick, a trash can, a pipe, whatever you can find.

HOW TO THWART A KIDNAPPING ATTEMPT

Abductions happen all over the world and for a myriad of reasons, from ransom, politics, and religion to sexual slavery and sexual predators. The best time to escape an abduction attempt is right when it happens. It is imperative that you maintain your situational awareness and do not panic. As always, you should start by taking preventive measures and making yourself a hard target.

PRE-PLANNING

- Always carry a cell phone with you.
- Stay aware of your surroundings at all times and avoid secluded areas like alleyways, backstreets, and barren parks.
- Purchase a personal alarm and keep it in your hand when you are walking through a questionable area; it may scare off a would-be abductor if activated.
- If it is legal in the country you are visiting, carry mace or a stun gun in your hand and know how to use it.

- When sitting, keep your back to the wall so that you can observe your surroundings.
- Always lock your doors at night and activate your home alarm system if you have one.
- When driving, keep your doors locked and windows rolled up at all times when traveling in an area that warrants such precautions.
- Listen to your gut. If you think you are in trouble and in risk of abduction, go directly to the police or the US embassy or call them on your cell phone.
- Plan for an abduction and think about what you would do if you were kidnapped. Play different scenarios out in your mind and visualize yourself taking action and what your different options are.
- What to do if abduction seems imminent: fight, flight, or cooperate

No two abduction attempts are the same, and for that reason it is important that you keep your wits about you, assess the situation, and come up with a plan of action. You need to refer back to your preparation phase of travel, where you studied the criminal and terrorist groups operating in the area that you are in. What is their most likely motivation for abducting you and what is their most likely course of action once they have you? If you are in South America, where abductions by paramilitary organizations are normally motivated by ransom collection and are almost always resolved with a prisoner release, then escape may not be the answer. If, however, you are in Iraq, Pakistan, or Afghanistan (for instance) and you are being abducted by groups associated with ISIS or Al-Qaeda, known for executing prisoners by beheading, you should make every effort to escape at your first opportunity.

FIGHT FOR YOUR LIFE

Fight for your safety as though your life depends on it, as that may very well be the case. Kicking, scratching, biting, small joint manipulation such as pulling back a pinky and breaking it, even grabbing onto stationary objects and not letting go, or using whatever you can find as a weapon to fight your abductor(s); anything you can do to get away is fair game.

Telegraphing eyes: While the mad or crazed look on your assailant's face can't harm you, his eyes can often give away his next move or others that he has helping him. The danger is in his hands but his eyes can telegraph a lot, so pay attention to both.

Don't forget the knees and feet: While eyes, ears, nose, throat, groin, and solar plexus are all sensitive areas that should be locked in on when defending yourself, the knees and feet are vulnerable areas as well and should not be overlooked. You can shatter a knee cap with about seven to ten pounds of pressure. The foot has many small bones in it that can easily be broken with a well-placed foot stomp.

WHAT TO DO AFTER YOU GET AWAY

For escape attempts, do whatever you have to do even if you may get hurt in the process. If you are thrown into a car, try to open the door on the other side of the car immediately, as the door is often left unlocked to allow another kidnapper to enter from the far side of the vehicle. If possible, you can use your feet and the strength of your legs to kick out the rear window and then throw yourself out of the vehicle and make a run for safety. If thrown into a van, attempt to use the momentum to power through the back doors. You may break a rib or dislocate a shoulder, but it may be better than what you would surely face in captivity. If nothing else, make a scene. Do not scream in a panic, it will only make the situation worse. Instead scream out commands such as "leave me alone!" or "call the police!" This technique works particularly well when you are near other people who can come to your aid or contact the police.

Always be ready to be ready: The average man can run twenty-one feet in about 1.5 seconds. That means that when a potential assailant is twenty-one feet away, you have 1.5 seconds to react.

This is why it is so important to be aware of what is going on around you. That does not mean you can't enjoy yourself or let your guard down, it just means you have to have situational awareness or that "sixth sense" to let you know when you need to be prepared to react. This will come through education and experience.

SEXUAL ASSAULT PREVENTION

Photo Credit: GettyImages

Sexual assault is a real threat for women and children both here in the United States and abroad. Below I have listed a few things you can do to lower the risk of this happening to you or to a loved one:

- Get your CCP and *always* carry a firearm. Ensure you are trained and ready to use it.
- Be alert. Don't assume that you are always safe. Think about your safety everywhere. Your best protection is avoiding dangerous situations.
- Carry a taser, stun gun, mace, or another less than lethal

weapon on your key chain and have it at the ready anytime you are walking alone.

- Trust your instincts. If you feel uncomfortable in any situation, leave.
- Always walk, drive, and park your car in well-lit areas.
- Walk confidently at a steady pace on the side of the street facing traffic.
- Walk close to the curb. Avoid doorways, bushes, and alleys.
- Wear clothes and shoes that allow freedom of movement.
- Walk to your car with keys in your hand.
- If you have car trouble, raise the hood and stay inside your car. If a stranger wants to help, have him or her call for help. Don't leave your car.
- Keep your car doors locked and never pick up hitchhikers.
- Make sure all windows and doors in your home are locked, especially if you are home alone.
- Never give the impression that you are home alone if strangers telephone or come to the door.
- If a stranger asks to use your phone, have him wait outside while you make the call.
- If you come home and find a door or window open or signs of forced entry, don't go in. Go to the nearest phone and call 911 if in the US or Post 1 or the local law enforcement authorities if overseas.

ACTIVE SHOOTER DEFENSE: WHAT TO DO IN THE EVENT OF WORKPLACE VIOLENCE, SCHOOL SHOOTINGS, AND OTHER INDISCRIMINATE MASS BLOODSHED

The world we live in is a dangerous place. The possibility of violence happening in the workplace is a real and present danger. In 1999, twelve students and one teacher were shot and killed at Columbine High School in Littleton, Colorado; an additional twenty-four students were injured. In 2012, twenty-six people were shot and killed and twenty-four additional students were injured at Sandy Hook Elementary School in Newtown, Connecticut. The

Photo Credit: GettyImages

Photo Credit: GettyImages

likelihood of one of these incidents happening again in the future is likely. Regardless of what the shooter's motivation is, be it a mental condition, a disgruntled employee, or a terrorist, it is imperative that you know the proper signs to look for, precautions to take, and what your actions should be in the event of an active-shooter scenario taking place.

LOOK FOR THE SIGNS

Start by using your situational awareness to identify pre-attack signs that something is wrong, such as:

- Signs of aggression or threats directed at coworkers or supervisors
- Existence of unapproved weapons
- Severe mood swings
- Depression/withdrawn behavior
- Talks of suicide
- Paranoia
- Strange behavior such as flashbacks
- Drug and alcohol abuse
- Repeated violation of policies in the work place
- Talk of personal problems such as marriage or finances

It is not always possible to predict an active shooter incident and not everyone who exhibits these signs is a potential active shooter. These are just situations to be sensitive of and to notice when someone displays one or multiple signs. In any case, you should report this behavior to your supervisors or to the local authorities, depending on the severity of the situation. Doing nothing is rarely the right answer.

HOW TO RESPOND

If you find yourself in an active shooter situation, you have several options regarding how to respond. Your first choice should always be to help others to evacuate the area. If there is an opportunity to evacuate, make sure you:

- Have a plan: Make sure you have an escape route in mind before you move

- Leave your belongings, they will just slow you down
- Help others escape, if possible
- Prevent other people from going near the area where the active shooter incident is happening
- Call 911 immediately
- Go out in the direction first responders are coming in
- Do exactly what the police officers tell you to do and keep your hands visible. Evacuating the area may not always be an option. If you find yourself unable to evacuate, consider finding a place to hide. The location you choose should:
  - » Be out of the view of the people or person doing the shooting
  - » Provide good cover (be able to deflect bullets fired in your direction), such as a concrete wall
  - » Have an escape route if possible/try not to box yourself in
  - » Have doors that lock from the inside
  - » Have heavy objects like furniture to block the door. Remember to put your cell phone on silent and hide behind the largest items you can find in your location. Stay calm, cool, and collected, and call 911 as soon as you get the chance.

TAKING ACTION

In a worst-case scenario, you may find yourself having to take physical action against the shooter. This is a very difficult situation, particularly if not trained and conditioned in the art of hand-to-hand combat. Still, it may be your last resort in a desperate situation and when innocent people are dying. If this is the case, remember to:

- Have a plan
- Commit to your actions 100 percent
- Be as aggressive as possible
- Improvise weapons if you can find any . . . throw large objects if they are available

- Get others to help you incapacitate the shooter if possible . . . several grown men can often combine their strength to tackle down a lone shooter Taking action against an armed aggressor is extremely risky but it may be your (or those you are responsible for) only chance of survival.

WHAT TO DO WHEN THE POLICE ARRIVE

One of the most dangerous times during an active shooter scenario is when first responders arrive. It is extremely confusing for them to differentiate between the victims and the perpetrators when these incidents take place. The best thing you can do when you make contact with the police is to:

- Stay calm and follow the instructions of the police
- If practical, find a corner to go to and keep low.
- Put down anything you may have in your hands
- Raise hands high in the sky so they can be seen by the police and keep them there
- Don't make any quick or jerking movements
- Avoid screaming and yelling. Maintain your situational awareness so that you will be able to provide the police with:
  - » Location of the shooter(s)
  - » Number of shooters
  - » Description of the shooter(s)
  - » Type of weapon used by the shooter(s)
  - » Estimated number of casualties

Photo credit: GettyImages

Travel Smart: How to Lower Your Risk of Becoming a Criminal or Terrorist Target at Home and Abroad

Photo Credit: GettyImages

Always be aware of your surroundings, especially in unfamiliar areas. Don't get into a situation where you are vulnerable. Photo Credit: GettyImages

Don't be too hard on the TSA; they are a "necessary evil" if you want to lower the risk of being the victim of a terrorist attack. Photo Credit: GettyImages

Criminals are known to target money exchanges at airports when looking for a "mark," which is a person that has something they both want and believe they can easily get. You are better off going to your personal bank before traveling and get the foreign cash from them. If it is an odd currency, then give your bank a day or so to get it for you. This way you not only won't target yourself, but you will most likely get a better exchange rate as well. Photo Credit: GettyImages

DO YOUR RESEARCH: IT WILL PAY DIVIDENDS TO YOUR SECURITY WHEN YOU TRAVEL ABROAD

In order to mitigate risk, you must first try to anticipate threats and hazards in the areas to which you plan to travel. Prior to traveling to a new and unfamiliar destination or to an area where the threat situation is fluid and has a history of changing quickly and without warning, it is important that you monitor the status and atmospherics on the ground before you enter into the travel phase of your plan. By taking these steps, you are sure to enhance personal security and the safety of others with whom you are traveling. It is possible to research criminal and terrorist activity by reading local newspapers on the Internet, or monitoring police reports in the prospective area of travel. A great resource for overseas travel is the United States Department of State's Travel Advisory website (https://travel.state. gov). Additionally, it is important to understand the techniques, tactics, and procedures of terrorist and criminal elements in areas where you plan to travel so you can have the highest level of situational awareness and best diminish your risk of becoming a target. Once you are able to identify the threat, it is less problematic to take the appropriate security measures to lower your overall risk of becoming a target. Plan to avoid high-risk areas while traveling or conduct appropriate safety procedures in the event that these areas are unavoidable.

KEEP YOUR HEAD ON A SWIVEL

It is imperative to remain vigilant at all times. The first step in remaining vigilant is to examine and understand your own pattern of living and daily environments. Once a "normal" pattern is established and identified, it will be much easier to recognize when something is out of place. Suspicious activities, such as an unknown person following or watching your daily movements, will tend to stand out when you are familiar with local routine patterns of life. You can obtain this knowledge by simply spending time observing the local area from a vantage point like the balcony of a hotel room or a park bench. A key indicator that a terrorist attack is imminent is when the local flow of life significantly decreases in an area where people are normally abundant. Remember to remain vigilant, keep your head on a swivel, and always report suspicious activity to local authorities if possible.

TURN YOURSELF INTO A HARD TARGET

You cannot always predict when a terrorist attack is going to occur or when you might become the target of a crime. Because of this, you should take steps to become a "hard" target—a target that terrorists and criminals would be likely to avoid due to the physical difficulty or material costs involved in engaging this particular target.

This may be accomplished by taking some simple steps, such as trying to be the "gray man" and trying to blend into your environment. For example, dress like the locals if that is feasible and practical. Do not wear clothing or jewelry that will make you visibly stand out in a crowd. Be as low key as possible. In other words, do not act like the stereotypical loud and vulgar "ugly American."

Furthermore, you should avoid known areas of high crime whenever possible and travel with a partner or in a small group.

Another risk-mitigating step that you may take is to avoid setting patterns in your own behavior. Try to be unpredictable. Take different routes to and from daily locations. Stay in the open and try to avoid dark alleys and areas that do not seem to be safe. Most of all, listen to your "sixth sense," the inner voice that we all have—your gut feelings. If something seems wrong, it probably is, so avoid it or proceed with great caution.

On top of having a solid grasp of the crime and terrorism threats that you may be faced with, it is also important to learn about the local government's attitude and response toward crime and terrorism before traveling. When you travel overseas, you must often rely on the government of the country you are visiting to protect you. Knowing this information will increase your situational awareness.

If you plan to travel abroad, be it for business, pleasure, or both, there are safety and security precautions and practices that you can implement both prior to traveling outside of the United States and while you are traveling to ensure that you have a smooth and enjoyable journey while avoiding the dangers, hassles, and inconveniences of a poorly planned trip.

TIPS ON THINGS TO BE DONE LONG BEFORE YOU DEPART

- You should update all of your records prior to traveling overseas and make sure that everything is in order in the event of an emergency.
- Get a good guide book and familiarize yourself with local food, customs, laws, and people.
- Contact the State Department's website and look for travel advisories.
- Get a good pocket phrase book and memorize several key phrases if you do not already speak the language. Keep the book with you when you travel. Smart Phone Apps are great but always keep a paper book as well; batteries run low and electronics malfunction but books don't.
- Get the contact information for the local embassy or

consulate in the country you are visiting. You can find that information on the State Department website as well.

- If you are using a travel agent, find out from them which airlines, car rental company, and hotel to use; they often have inside information on these things.
- Don't forget to update your passport, get your visa, and have your shot records updated long before your day of departure.
- Visas can take weeks to months or longer to obtain depending on what country it is you wish to travel to and your reason for going.

Note: Make sure that you check your passport to ensure that there is no information in it that could get you into trouble in the country you are traveling to. For instance, if visiting an Islamic country, it is not advisable to have an Israeli stamp in your passport booklet.

TIPS ON PACKING AND LUGGAGE

Don't be the person who is too cheap to rent a cart or to check in their luggage, so they fumble their way trough the airport carrying a ton of luggage and lose all sense of what is going on around them. These are the signs that bad guys use to mark you as an easy target to exploit. Instead, try to pack as light as you can and check in any luggage you can, keeping only your most important gear and documents with you in the cabin including a change of clothing and some toiletries for that "just in case" moment when the airline loses your luggage. Photo Credit: GettyImages

- Pack as light as possible. People who carry an abundant amount of unnecessary luggage tend to target themselves to criminals as inexperienced travelers and therefore naïve to criminal tricks, ruses, and ploys. It also makes you a slow moving target.

- Choose luggage that is durable, easily recognizable, and subdued in color so as not to make you stand out in a crowd when carrying it. If you want to make it stand out so it is not confused with someone else's luggage, tie a bandana to it or purchase a fluorescent handle wrap.

- Avoid military-style luggage such as aviator kit bags and dufflebags; they will only target you as being affiliated with the military. Take only what is necessary.

- Choose items that can play dual roles; the more things one item does well, the fewer overall items you need to carry.

- Pack at least a thirty-day supply of extra prescription medication in your check-in luggage and make sure you have the proof of prescription information with you.

if you have an uncommon size shoe, don't expect to always be able to pick up another pair at your final destination. it is always better to take what you need with you just in case. Photo Credit: GettyImages

- Choose clothes that are light and versatile. Know the weather in the country you are visiting and pack accordingly. If it is a business trip, don't assume that you will not have to visit some remote locations where some more rugged clothing may be a better choice than a suit and tie.
- Always put an extra pair of comfortable clothing and a toiletry kit as well as at least a week's supply of any needed medication, and all of your important documents into a carry-on bag that you keep with you at all times.

Note: If you have special clothing needs, if you are an unusual cut such as XXXL or very tall, or if you have a particularly small, large, or wide foot, it would be a mistake to assume that any clothing you forgot to bring can be acquired during your travels. I can tell you that I have wasted an incredible amount of time trying on shoes to fit my 13EEE foot to no avail! If you require an uncommon wardrobe item, be sure that you bring it with you from the states and make certain that you don't lose it or you may find yourself having to pay an unmentionable amount of money to have the item shipped to your location.

- If you are bringing a carry-on, make sure baggage will fit easily in the carry-on baggage compartment (approximately 22" x 14" x 9" or 56 x 35 x 23 cm).
- If you are carrying a laptop, make sure it is easily accessible for security check points.

Note: Check your computer to ensure that it is free and clear of anything that may be considered illegal or contraband in the country you are traveling to (such as pornography or even political and religious documents).

- On your check-in and carry-on luggage, ensure that you conceal your nametag so that it does not advertise your name, address, and/or company affiliation. Put another identification tag or index card inside of your check-in luggage in the event that the ID tag on your luggage is lost.

TIPS ON WHAT NOT TO PUT IN YOUR CARRY-ON LUGGAGE

Photo Credit: GettyImages

Know what is considered contraband in the country you are traveling to and do not pack it in your luggage. You can find out what items not to bring to any given country by contacting the State Department website or the embassy, or from researching those countries' restrictions on the web. According to the Transportation Safety Administration, the following items are restricted in your carry-on luggage:

- Sharp objects
- Sporting goods
- Firearms
- Tools
- Martial arts and self-defense items
- Explosive and flammable materials, disabling chemicals, and other dangerous items

TIPS ON THINGS TO BE DONE DAYS BEFORE YOU DEPART

Before your day of travel, you should definitely let someone know where you are going, and you should give that trusted individual access to your important files such as:

- Itinerary (starting with travel to your destination, write down everywhere you plan to go and a basic timeline . . . be as detailed as possible)
- Power of attorney (for relatives or spouse)
- Birth certificates
- Marriage certificates
- Proof of insurance
- Medical history and records
- Finances/bills
- Credit card number and expiration date
- Social Security number
- Bank account information (bank name, account number and routing number)
- Passport photocopy (get every page) and a duplicate passport photo in event passport needs to be replaced
- Two recent pictures; one frontal and one profile
- DNA sample (hair with follicle, pin prick of blood, or a sample of saliva)
- Fingerprints (put on blank paper and label each finger)
- Phone numbers/emails/ways to contact you while you are away
- Points of contact in the country your traveling to (if you have them)
- Address and phone number list of all family members and close friends

TIPS ON THINGS TO CONSIDER ON THE DAY OF TRAVEL

- Dress like the natives. Don't wear clothing that will target you or make you stand out from everyone else on your flight.
- Don't wear jewelry or have accessories that will target you as being someone of high stature or wealth. Avoid wearing exposed religious medallions, as they will only further target you.
- Shoes that are practical for walking long distances are a must-have item. Shoes should also be easy to take off and put back on during security checks.
- Put a note card in your wallet with emergency contact information, your current medications, your insurance information, your blood type, and any allergies that you may have. Write anything else on the card that you can think of that may be useful in an emergency where you cannot speak for yourself.
- Carry a phone number list with consulate and embassy contact numbers on it.
- Make sure you have your tickets, your passport, another form of ID such as a driver's license, and your visa for the country you are traveling to.
- Make sure you have a current copy of your shot records and ensure that you are up to date on the shots needed to visit the country you are traveling to.

TIPS ON MONEY AND OTHER FORMS OF CURRENCY

- Go to your local bank and get a few hundred dollars in small bills in the currency of the country you are traveling to and put it in your wallet before traveling. Criminals are known to stake out currency exchanges in airports to see who takes out large withdrawals. You can avoid this by already having money on you.
- You should carry a Visa or MasterCard credit card with at

Photo Credit: GettyImages

least a few thousands dollar credit limit on it and a modest
amount of money in the form of travelers checks.

• It never hurts to have 100 dollars or so in American (US)
cash as well . . . it still talks loud in many countries.

TIPS FOR CREDIT CARD USE

• Be sure to call your credit card company and let them know
where you are traveling to and the dates. If you do not, there
is a good possibility that they will shut down your card as
soon as it is used overseas, as their fraud department will
almost surely be alerted. It can be a hassle to get the card
reactivated once they shut it down.

• Be aware of the most widely used credit card scams such as
photo images captured, hackers, fake card readers or fake
ATM faces, and the plethora of other scams perpetrated
every day.

• Only use credit cards that offer theft insurance and call your

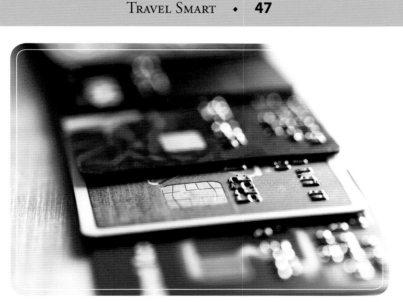

Photo Credit: GettyImages

card company to make sure it is covered in the country you are traveling to.

- Keep a note someplace secure other than your wallet with your credit card information on it as well as the number to call if your card is lost or stolen.

TIPS FOR PHONE USE OVERSEAS

- Call your phone company and see about getting an international plan and data package for your trip. This way you can use your phone for emergencies overseas without being hammered with the most expensive international rates.
- Consider buying a phone as soon as you get into the country you are traveling to and purchasing individual minute cards.
- Remember, you never know who is listening to your calls, so be careful not to divulge personal or sensitive information over the phone when traveling abroad.

Photo Credit: GettyImages

TRAVEL CULTURAL AWARENESS TIP

- Be aware of the culture of the country you are traveling to so as not to offend anyone. If you are traveling to an Islamic country and you are a female, for instance, consider covering your neck and the back of your head. In many Asian

Photo Credit: GettyImages

countries it is customary to remove your shoes before going into someone's home.

- Even the US has do's and don'ts; for example, a woman going topless on a public beach in the United States would be considered indecent while doing so in most European countries is perfectly normal. Every culture has its own customs and courtesies that you would be prudent to take into consideration.

TIPS TO HELP WITH AIRLINE SELECTION AND THE RESERVATION PROCESS

Photo Credit: GettyImages

- If you are not flying on a US airline, then remember your ABCs (Australia, Britain, and Canada) when deciding who to fly with, as they possess the best track records for safety.
- If feasible, try to book non-stop flights or flights with as few connections as possible.
- If possible, when traveling outside of the US, avoid small local airlines or at least try and ask around or research which airlines have the best safety record.
- Selecting a seat toward the front of the aircraft will get you on the plane quicker and you will be the first to get off the plane once you arrive as well.

Note: When hijacking or aircraft malfunction is a consideration, seat selection is tricky; window seats will limit your exposure in the event of a hijacking, but it will also limit your ability to help in the event that you are needed. A window seat in coach located in an emergency exit row is generally considered the safest place to sit from a hijacked aircraft perspective or in an emergency where you had to quickly evacuate the aircraft.

TIPS FOR A SMOOTH ARRIVAL TO THE AIRPORT AND GETTING TO THE TERMINALS

- Try to arrive at the airport at least two hours prior to your scheduled departure time. If you are in a rush, you are bound to forget something and you do not leave room for small issues that may arise.
- In order to avoid exposure time to unsecure areas, you want to get through security and into the main terminal as quickly as possible. To do this, have all of your important documents readily available.
- Never leave your bags unattended or carry anything for anyone you do not know.
- You can often check in online a day in advance of your flight and choose your seat at the same time. Printing your boarding passes ahead of time will prevent you from having to stand in line for self-check in and allow you to move directly to the ticket counter.

TIPS FOR GETTING THROUGH AIRPORT SECURITY

- Be prepared to be searched thoroughly.
- Wearing shoes that easily slip on and off, belts with plastic buckles, minimal jewelry or other metallic items, and having your laptop computer already out of its carrying case prior to getting up to security will make getting through the security point a much easier and more flowing experience.
- Consider signing up for the TSA PreCheck program (http://travelprecheck.org/expedited/screening).

Photo Credit: GettyImages

- About 30 percent of passengers can be expected to be pulled aside for further searching. This is most likely not because you look like a terrorist. There is a security search quota that must be met and then there are always going to be times when either one of the sensitive sensing devises goes off mistakenly, or you had an item in your carry-on luggage that the X-ray tech could not recognize. Just be cooperative and polite and you will be back on your way in no time.
- From the time you pack your luggage to the time you get on the plane (or check in your luggage with the airline), do not let your bags get out of your positive control.
- Know exactly what you have in your luggage and on your person and be prepared to explain those items to security personnel.
- Do not say anything that will cause you to be held up by security, even if you are only joking. Words such as "bomb," "explosives," or "gun" can easily cause you to be detained by security personnel. This could cause you to miss your flight, face fines, and even be imprisoned depending on the laws of the country you are in.
- When boarding your flight, be kind and courteous to

security and airline personnel; they are there to help you and being a disgruntled passenger can only make things worse for you.

SECURITY TIPS FOR AIR PASSENGERS

Photo Credit: GettyImages

- Listen carefully to the flight attendant's safety instructions and understand the procedures for evacuating the aircraft.
- Be aware of your surroundings and be aware of the personal information you give out while having a conversation with the passenger next to you, because you never know who else is listening.
- When traveling from one overseas destination to another, avoid speaking English in a loud voice whenever possible so as not to advertise yourself as an American.
- Be discreet and maintain your situational awareness.

TIPS FOR RENTING A CAR AT THE AIRPORT OR IN YOUR DESTINATION LOCATION

Photo Credit: GettyImages

- Many people choose to reserve their rental cars at the same time they make their airline reservations. If you plan to reserve a car in the country you are traveling to, make sure you are fully prepared to drive in the environment you are visiting.
- You must call or contact the embassy to see what the driving restrictions are and if you need an international driving permit for the country you are visiting.
- If you do need an international driving permit, you can get one by going to the AAA website at http://www.aaa.com.
- Know the name of the car rental company, the license plate number, year, make, model, and VIN number of your rental vehicle. Keep this information in your wallet. If your vehicle is stolen, you will have the pertinent information needed by the local police to try and recover your vehicle.

HOTEL SELECTION

Photo Credit: GettyImages

You can take several precautionary measures to lower the possibility of becoming a target in a hotel, starting with hotel selection. Try to find lodgings in a low-crime area. Hotels that feature security cameras in the lobby, halls, and on the outside are positive choices. Try to find modern hotels that offer electronic key card entry to rooms and to side doors. Hotels should have a central lobby where all who are not guests must pass in order to enter the facility. You should seek to stay in hotels that have security guards and hotel staff on duty round-the-clock because they provide a high level of security. You may never find a hotel overseas with all of these characteristics, but they are good markers to look for when inquiring about a place to stay.

Additionally, hotels that have solid doors on the rooms are ideal because they are likely to provide a deterrent against an intruder and make a more efficient barricade in the event of a terrorist attack.

ROOM SELECTION

Try to choose a room on the third, fourth, or fifth floor of the hotel. Anything lower than the third floor and the rooms are too easily accessible to thieves and criminals. Anything higher than the fifth floor and emergency service personnel might have a difficult time gaining the access they require. If crime in the area is a concern, avoid rooms with balconies. Locks on balcony doors are normally much easier to circumvent and criminals often use balconies to get from room to room. Look for rooms midway between emergency exits if possible; rooms directly next to emergency exits are often-times targeted for theft. You should not choose a room too far away from an emergency exit in the event that evacuation from the building is necessary. Ask for a room that does not have an interior that opens to an adjacent room. Finally, look for hotels with rooms that open to the hotel interior. Exterior room entrances may provide less protection and less observation by hotel staff.

Hotel key: Keep your room key with you at all times. If the key has a room number on it, don't display it for everyone to see. Never leave your room key lying on a bar or table.

HOTEL SECURITY

Criminal activity in and around hotels is also a threat that travelers will face both in the United States and abroad. Thieves, and others who wish to do harm, will use various tactics to gain access to hotel rooms. These tactics include, but are not limited to, following

Photo Credit: GettyImages

individuals and their family members and then forcing their way into hotel rooms to gain access to valuables. They may also create the appearance of hotel staff to gain access to rooms or slip into the rooms when the legitimate hotel staff is servicing those rooms.

DON'T BE PREDICTABLE

Avoid setting predictable patterns when staying in hotels located in high crime locations. You can achieve this by changing room numbers when arriving to the hotel just in case someone has checked the room number from the reservation. If you feel you may be at a greater risk of targeting, change hotel rooms every few days to deter would-be thieves or criminals. Once inside the hotel room, be sure to conduct a thorough room inspection. Check the telephone to make sure it works and test all the doors and windows to ensure working locks. Look for a security peephole in the door and identify nearby emergency exits. You must attempt to make yourself more difficult to recognize by blending in with people and surroundings in and around the hotel. Always have emergency numbers at hand, such as those for the front desk, the local authorities, and the American Consulate. Make a plan detailing what each member of your party must do in the event of an emergency and make sure it includes good rallying points or places to go, both inside and outside of the hotel. If traveling with others, make sure everyone understands where to meet in the event of an emergency. Do not be predictable or set up patterns. If your room is on the third floor, occasionally take the elevator to the fifth or sixth floor and walk down a few flights of stairs to avoid being followed by others. Do not open the door to unexpected strangers; call the front desk and confirm names of hotel staff if you are unsure of the identity of a visitor. Maintain positive control of room keys. When leaving the hotel room, make it appear as though someone is still in room by leaving the television and/or lights on, and keeping the "Do Not Disturb" sign on the door. If the room needs cleaning, make sure not to leave any valuables or paperwork lying around. Always lock valuables in the hotel safe.

CRIME AWARENESS AND PREVENTION WHEN TRAVELING ABROAD

When traveling, always be aware of your surroundings. Photo Credit: GettyImages

Situational awareness is a key factor in not making yourself a target. Understand your environment and then act accordingly. For example, if you are traveling to a high crime area, where pickpocketing is the preferred method of theft, then you should take steps to avoid the risk of being pickpocketed. Avoid crowds, if possible, keeping your wallet in a front pocket and possibly even attaching your wallet to a pants pocket or belt with a lanyard, thereby lowering the risk of being pickpocketed. Avoid digging through a purse or wallet and counting money in public. Consider taking out small bills and putting them in a front pocket if you need to purchase souvenirs or other simple items. Further, it is important to keep your wallet in a safe and secure location on your body. Some people even choose to construct a "mugger's wallet" by taking an old wallet and putting a couple of small bills and even a couple of expired credit cards in it and placing this as a decoy in their back pocket. That way, if you are mugged or pickpocketed, the criminals will not get away with anything of value. If you wear a purse, make sure the strap is long enough to wear diagonally across your chest. Many people choose to wear a backpack when traveling or sightseeing. If you wear a backpack, never leave valuables where they are easily accessible from the rear. When walking through areas highly congested with people, consider wearing a backpack in front of the body if feasible, particularly if you are in a high crime area.

AREAS TO AVOID AT NIGHT

When it comes to crime, time is a key factor. What I mean by this is that while crime may be a 24/7 occurrence, crimes do follow somewhat of a pattern statistically. For instance, while most business break-ins and personal assaults happen late at night when there are the fewest people awake and able to witness the crime, residential break-ins mainly occur during the day when people are normally away from their homes. The point is that understanding the criminal activity "biorhythm" will give you a much better understanding of what areas to avoid and when to avoid them.

CRIME PREVENTION TIPS FOR TRAVELERS

Always make copies of your important documents. Photo Credit: GettyImages

It is never anyone's intention to have their business trip or vacation interrupted by a theft but these things do happen, so there are some things that you can do to minimize your risk and to make the situation as manageable as possible:

- Always have a legible photocopy of your passport, airline tickets, credit cards, and anything else that you think would be difficult to replace if it was ever stolen. Keep this in a separate location away from your wallet.
- Keep a list of your credit card companies' phone numbers (away from your wallet) so you can call them immediately if your cards get stolen.

TIPS TO PREVENT THEFT

- Keep your large sums of money as well as credit cards in your front trouser pocket or in a zipped compartment or pocket.
- If you have to carry a wallet in an unbuttoned pocket, only carry in it what you can afford to lose.
- Attach your keys to a loop on your clothing.
- Don't pat your pocket to see if your wallet is still there while in public; this only lets criminals know the exact location of your wallet if they are watching you.
- Women should choose a purse that is hard to open, such as one with a zipper.
- Purses should have a long enough strap to be worn horizontally across back.

HOW TO PREVENT THEFT FROM YOUR VEHICLE

The most common type of theft is the theft of valuables from an automobile. This is generally a crime of opportunity and it most often happens when valuables are left in plain sight.

- Keep valuables like cell phones, radar detectors, wallets, and briefcases out of sight.

- When shopping, if you plan to leave your vehicle, place your purchased items in the trunk.
- CD's are another item that can trigger a theft; keep them out of view, such as in a compartment or center console.
- Keep your car doors locked and your windows up at all times when you are away from your vehicle.

HOW TO AVOID AND DETECT TERRORIST AND CRIMINAL SURVEILLANCE

Photo Credit: GettyImages

Terrorists and criminals conduct surveillance to obtain information about either a stationary target or an individual so that they may create a more specific plan to execute their attack. If they are criminals, this helps them to determine the most opportune time to perform their theft or other crime. Normally, when surveillance is conducted against an individual, it is to ascertain what security measures are in place in and around their home, what vehicles they drive, when people come and go, and the level of the target's situational awareness (i.e., are you a hard or soft target?).

WHO IS THE TARGET OF SURVEILLANCE?

Terrorists and criminals conduct surveillance against stationary targets like facilities and other infrastructure to determine guard patterns, first responder reaction times, facility security measures, and shift rotations. Detecting terrorist or criminal surveillance is the key to lowering the likelihood of an attack or a crime being committed. If you notice someone conducting surveillance on a specific facility, building, or any piece of infrastructure, you should contact local authorities immediately.

HOW SURVEILLANCE IS CONDUCTED

When people conduct surveillance, they generally attempt to blend into their environment. Watch for the telltale signs of nefarious surveillance activities, such as unknown personnel in a stationary position like a car parked for an extended amount of time. Also, try to notice suspicious activities like people taking multiple pictures or videos of buildings or structures, taking notes, or drawing sketches. You should look for people paying an inordinate amount of time and attention to things that would not usually demand much attention. Criminals/terrorists may also try to blend into their environment by doing something ordinary like reading a newspaper or looking at a cell phone. Terrorists and criminals may also use members of the opposite sex to gain information. Be aware of people asking prying questions. Beware of electronic surveillance, as well. If you suspect that electronic surveillance devices, or "bugs," are present, do not speak freely until you dispose of the listening device or leave the area.

WHAT TO DO IF YOU SUSPECT YOU ARE UNDER CRIMINAL OR TERRORIST SURVEILLANCE

If the situation is static, meaning you are in a stationary location, and you suspect that you have been "marked" or selected by a criminal or terrorist as either a preplanned target or simply a target of opportunity, the best thing you can do is to use your cell phone to immediately alert the authorities and to make your way to either the local police or to the American embassy or one of our allies. In more kinetic settings, where you suspect you are being followed either in a vehicle, or on foot, then you can assume there is more than one person involved, since this type of surveillance is normally conducted by teams. That said, your first reaction of alerting the authorities is the same. Don't assume that just because no one is visibly behind you that you are not being followed. In some cases you may have been under observation for some time while those watching you learned your normal pattern of life. Once those conducting surveillance learn your routes, they will use that knowledge to their advantage. They may not even be following behind their intended subject, but by anticipating the route, they may have cars or people all along the subject's intended route. You should also not count out the possibility of the use of ROV's (Remotely Operated Vehicles, such as drones), aircraft, and even satellite technology, depending on the sophistication of those on your tail.

HOW TO LOSE A TAIL

First, you must determine if there is an individual or team following along your route. You can do this by varying your pace and noting

If you think you are being followed, try to move towards a populated area.
Photo Credit: GettyImages

if the potential follower varies his/her pace, turning in the opposite direction to see if they still follow, or stopping to tie your shoe in front of a store window to see the reaction of any person that may be following.

If driving a car, you can make several turns off the intended route to see if the "tail" follows. If on foot and you determine that there is another person following, continue to walk, and as always, if possible, call the police and alert them to the situation.

Once you are sure another person is following, make a mental note of what the follower looks like. Try to speed up and duck out of sight. Once you are out of sight, do everything possible to change your own appearance. If wearing a jacket, take it off. The same applies to hats and or sunglasses or even eyeglasses. Do whatever is possible to look different from what the follower is expecting. Once changed in appearance, you should continue moving quickly. Go into a crowded area like a shopping market and then immediately go out through another exit. Go upstairs and through hallways, doubling back occasionally. Try to confuse those attempting to follow. As an absolute final option, you should hide somewhere that decreases the likelihood of discovery and wait awhile before going back out again. Other things you can do to lose a tail are:

- Buy a movie ticket to a show that already started. Go into the theater and out the emergency exit before your pursuer has a chance to follow you.
- Go into a restaurant or storefront and out through the back exit.
- Use reflective surfaces to see behind you, like the reflection in a store window.
- Use public transportation like getting on a train or bus just before the doors close. Be cautious with this technique, because if your follower makes it onto the mass transit platform you are stuck with him until the vehicle stops again.
- Always head toward crowds and try to avoid moving in the direction of seclusion. There is safety in numbers and the

more people you blend yourself into, the harder it will be for someone to follow you.

- Remember, never head for home or to a place that your follower may already know about. Assume that your pursuer has this information. Go straight to the police, the US Consulate, or the US Embassy.

EVASIVE DRIVING TECHNIQUES

Photo Credit: GettyImages

Imagine you are in downtown Chicago on a business trip during a time when a particularly volatile and highly contested murder trial involving a Chicago Police Officer and a deceased alleged gang member is taking place. The verdict is finally read in favor of the police officer, and what was at first peaceful protest quickly erupts into rioting, pandemonium, and all-out chaos. Cars are set on fire; store fronts are smashed open with bricks and then looted and set ablaze; and anyone who even resembles a law-abiding citizen is in grave danger. At the same moment hundreds of similar protests that had been building in size and intensity in cities all across the nation burst out into violence as well. It may appear as if all of this happened spontaneously, and without any premeditated planning or preparation, but in reality the entire thing was well planned out as an orchestrated act of civil disobedience and violence master-minded by a group of people who are dedicated to destroying our nation from within. They are backed logistically and financially by foreign entities that have similar motives. What are you going to do? You know you need to distance yourself from this reckless display of indiscriminate rage, but it seems hopeless as hostile mobs armed with baseball bats, rocks, and Molotov cocktails are met by huge plumes of tear gas and the intense stings of rubber bullets employed by the outnumbered contingent of law enforcement personnel. You finally make it to your vehicle and actually find your way down the spiral parking garage and into a side street. The problem is that there are people everywhere and none of them seem to be friendly. On top of that, in order for you to make it out of the city or at least to a part of the city still under control of the police, you will have to drive directly through areas that seem to be experiencing some of the worst rioting and chaos.

So . . . does this scenario seem too far-fetched to happen here in the United States? Did you know that not only is this type of scenario not improbable, but very similar occurrences have taken place right here in the United States. From the LA riots in the wake of the Rodney King verdict in 1992 to the riots and violence that took place across the nation after the Michael Brown shooting in Ferguson, Missouri in 2014; these things have happened many times in the past and you can be assured that they will happen again in the future. We live in a time where the country is divided and polarized along sociopolitical lines and more often than not you can expect people to turn to violence when they no longer feel that words are powerful enough to bring attention to whatever it is that they deem important. The question is, when this violence breaks out and if you find yourself caught in the middle of it, do you think you have the knowledge and skills to navigate through such chaos and violence in order to get yourself or your family to safety? Well, maybe you do, but it can't hurt to either learn new skills or to reinforce what you already know, and that is what this book is all about!

Note: Learning how to master evasive tactical driving skills cannot be done through reading alone. The best way to acquire these skills is to attend a professional evasive driving course where you can be trained by experienced instructors who are able to offer the proper terrain, obstacles, vehicles, and one-on-one training needed for you to become proficient at employing evasive driving techniques properly.

Note: A vehicle is a dangerous machine that has killed millions of people indiscriminately. According to the National Highway Transportation Safety Administration, there were over 40,000 vehicle-related deaths in the US alone in 2017. That's almost three times more people than those killed by guns in the US the same year! While it is important to understand that a vehicle can be used as a viable tool and even as a weapon to get you and your loved ones out of a really bad situation, it is important that you always remain cognizant of the lethal capabilities of a vehicle. Treat it with the same respect as you would a firearm.

Note: While this chapter is mainly about evasive driving and not marksmanship, I can't stress enough how important it is to your safety and the safety of your loved ones for you to not only own a firearm, but for you to become educated in using it. You should get to a point where using a firearm becomes second nature for you; as if your weapon is simply an extension of your body. Contrary to what many sharpshooting schools may claim, the only true way to become an expert with your firearm is to first learn proper form from an expert. Since not many people have had the privilege of serving with military special operations forces or with a police S.W.A.T unit, my suggestion would be for you to attend a civilian shooting school that is recognized for its professionalism and for the quality of instruction. A good place to start for the basics is the

National Rifle Association (NRA). The time to start training to use your weapon in a crisis is not when it is happening, but right now, before your life depends on your ability to employ it proficiently.

#1: HOW TO DRIVE THROUGH A RIOT WITHOUT BEING KILLED

Photo Credit: GettyImages

Before getting into the "how to," it is important to first understand what a "mob mentality" is. When people enter into what psychologists often call "group think," they no longer feel a sense of personal accountability for their actions. Now don't get me wrong: Entering into such behavior is a conscious decision and these people are liable for their actions, but when they get caught up in the group situation they lose sight of moral, ethical, and legal constraints. Taking the mob psychological factors into consideration, the most important thing to remember about driving through an angry mob of people is to *never* stop moving. That may seem easy enough, but the fact is that most human beings have had it hard wired into their brains since they first started driving that when you see people in front of you, you stop. The trick is to go slow but steady so that the crowd never sees any hesitation in your driving. It's basically a really slow game of chicken. If they even suspect that you may panic and stop if one of them were to run in front of your car, then someone will almost certainly call your bluff. Your hope is that once the crowd realizes that your vehicle is going to continue to move and slowly accelerate, then they will not chance trying to impede your movement and you will eventually be able to break out of the crowd. On the flip side, what you want to avoid is running over and either injuring or killing someone in the crowd, as it could actually backfire on you and cause someone to possibly jump onto your vehicle, smash your windows, or maybe even shoot you or drag you out of your vehicle and beat you to death. That is why I always say that you should avoid mobs at all cost when the opportunity presents itself, but sometimes you just don't have a choice and that is why I covered it here.

#2: KNOW HOW TO LOSE A TAIL IF YOU SUSPECT YOU ARE BEING FOLLOWED

If in a car and there is reason to believe you are being followed, your option is to turn on the vehicle's turn signal and then at the last second go straight and see if the other vehicle follows. Trying

Photo Credit: GettyImages

to outrun another vehicle is unsafe and will most likely only place innocent people in danger. Instead, drive sporadically; make left turns when signaling right turns, and go straight when indicating a turn. Slow down at a busy intersection just as the light changes. As soon as the light goes from yellow to red speed up and get through before the other cars have a chance to go. This technique will often leave your pursuers stranded at the light. Eventually, you will lose those who are following. If not, drive directly to the authorities or park the vehicle and then evade on foot and try to lose them. Again, if you think you are the target of surveillance by terrorists or criminals, promptly report these activities to the local police. Do not drive home or to a secluded area. If you suspect that the intent of the person or people following you is to do you harm, then you want to do everything you can to remain in highly populated areas. If the situation escalates, you should consider ditching your vehicle and evading your pursuer by cloaking your movement with a crowd and hiding any part of your appearance that stands out as you make your way to a police officer, police station, or anyone of authority who can offer you protection.

#3: KNOW HOW TO BREAK THROUGH VEHICLE BARRICADES AND ROAD BLOCKS

You should always assume that a barricade—be it one or more vehicles or some other object that is being used to obstruct vehicle movement through a particular route—is being observed by a person or a group of people who either do not want you to continue forward or who want to exploit or harm you in some way. Because of this, I would advise that you make it a point to do all that you can to either back up or turn around and find another access point to get to where you are going.

Understanding that there may be a time where turning around and avoiding a roadblock or barricade may not be an option, it is still important to understand the fundamentals of breaching these obstacles. Vehicular road blocks are somewhat more predictable and therefore easier than other road obstructions since they can

Photo Credit: GettyImages

often be breached if you ram them at the correct point. The object is to strike the vehicle at one of its two hard points at the axles, and strike it with one of your hard points along the frame, so basically you are hitting your headlights into the tire of the vehicle you want to move. The rear end of the blocking vehicle is your best choice, as it tends to be lighter than the front end where the engine is usually located. Your second choice would be the front end of the blocking vehicle. The bottom line is that the closer you ram into either end of a blocking vehicle, the better, understanding that the key is to avoid hitting the center of the blocking vehicle, since the closer you strike to the center of the vehicle the more weight you are pushing, until eventually you will just have a T-bone collision instead of a ram.

Things to remember when ramming:

- Never strike at more than 30 mph
- Never start more than three car lengths back
- Be careful when striking a vehicle that is significantly lower than your wheel and fender height
- If your vehicle gets fender locked, continue to accelerate

away and jiggle the steering wheel back and forth to break loose

Your ability to breach most roadblocks or barricades will be directly proportionate to who it is that is trying to stop you. If law enforcement or any other highly trained and equipped organization is trying to stop your movement, they will most likely succeed in doing so. The level of technology employed in both the lethal and non-lethal realm of specialized devices and systems aimed at disabling a target vehicle is incredibly advanced. Nets, spikes, foams, and even technology to shut off your engine are all available to those who can afford them. I suggest you pick your battles wisely.

#4: KNOW HOW TO CONDUCT A TACTICAL TURN AROUND

THREE-POINT TURN

Most obstacles and threats can be avoided by executing a basic three-point turn and either distancing yourself from a potential threat or finding another way to get to where you need to be. How you choose to turn around is a matter of choice and often depends on the circumstances and conditions, but out of all the methods for turning your vehicle around, the three-point turn is the safest and easiest to learn. It's the method of choice when you're in an area that isn't wide enough for you to simply do a U-turn to loop around to the opposite direction. To execute a three-point turn, you simply turn toward the left and move forward until you get up onto the edge of the opposite lane. Next turn the wheel all the way to the right and back up until you reach the edge of the side of the road that you started on. Finally, turn all the way back to the left and drive forward until you are facing in the opposite direction from which you started. Then you can quickly accelerate away from the obstacle, or suspected threat.

180-DEGREE TURNS

Note: The forward 180 (aka "Bootlegger") and reverse 180 turn (aka "J-Turn") are techniques used to quickly turn your vehicle in the opposite direction when faced with a threat to the front when there is not enough space to your left and right to allow you to turn around in a more traditional fashion. In the past these techniques were only taught to those in executive protection, security contracting, and those who work within specialized military units or government agencies. These days you will find many schools throughout the United States that offer training in these and other tactical driving maneuvers to anyone interested in learning how to perform them. On that note, do not try these moves at home! Both of these maneuvers can be quite rough on a vehicle and can be dangerous or even deadly if they are executed incorrectly. To mitigate risk while attempting to master these skills, you should seek out training by a tactical driving instructor and learn these techniques under controlled conditions.

The concept of the forward 180-turn technique seems simple enough. When you see the threat, lock your parking brake (this engages the rear breaking system of the vehicle) and your rear wheels will start sliding at that speed. Once the rear wheels start to slide, turn the steering wheel about a quarter turn toward the area with the least obstructions. This should cause your vehicle to rotate about 180 degrees, leaving you facing the opposite direction and ready to release the parking brake and speed away from the attack site.

Note: There are several variables that must all be working in your favor to successfully pull off one of these high-speed tactical reversal techniques. To perform a bootlegger turn, you need to be traveling at 35 to 40 mph; have four to five car lengths of distance left between yourself and the threat once you reach that speed; be on a hard, dry surface that is free of obstacles or obstructions; and not happen to be driving in a vehicle equipped with skid prevention systems (a challenge all in itself in 2019).

THE REVERSE 180 "J-TURN"

The idea behind the reverse 180 "J-Turn" is that it can be used when you don't have enough speed built up or distance between yourself and the threat to do a forward 180 turn and when you have a clear unobstructed path to your rear. A properly executed J-Turn would require you to come to a complete stop, put the vehicle in reverse, and then floor the gas pedal while keeping the vehicle in as straight a line as possible while counting to four seconds, which theoretically should put the vehicle at about 20 to 25 mph, giving you the needed momentum to complete the maneuver. Once you hit the four count, take your foot off the accelerator and turn the wheel as quickly as possible toward the open road or unobstructed area, locking the steering wheel at its limit. The violent and quick spinning of the front wheels will cause the front tires to lose their grip on the surface, causing the front of the vehicle to slide around, pivoting on the rear tires. As the vehicle is moving around in its arch, you will begin to rotate your steering wheel in a counter steer back to its original start. You should now be facing 180 degrees away from the attack. Quickly put your car into drive and move away from the threat as quickly as possible.

Note: Two things to remember if you ever do need to attempt a J-Turn: Never use your brakes during the reverse 180-degree turn, and do not have your foot on the gas as you are shifting the car back into drive, as this could cause severe damage your transmission and reduce your chances of escaping the threat.

Note: The fact is that these techniques are inherently dangerous and require a large amount of resources and practice to perfect. The vast majority of drivers out there do not have any of the required training to successfully pull off these maneuvers, unless you count on spending more than a few nights binge watching Vin Diesel movies; and it is this fact that exponentially increases your chances of rolling the vehicle and killing yourself and/or an innocent bystander when you attempt the technique.

Note: My advice to you is that if you need to back up in a hurry, simply place the vehicle in reverse and move out quickly. You can easily move hundreds of feet from any threat that has confronted you and thereby afford yourself a vital time buffer to allow you to decide on your next move, or to quickly execute a three-point turn and get away from the threat in question.

#5: KNOW WHAT TO DO WHEN SOMEONE TRIES TO RUN YOU OFF THE ROAD

Photo Credit: GettyImages

There is a technique known as the Precision Immobilization Technique, or P.I.T., that is used to immobilize another vehicle from behind. While the technique is most commonly used by law-enforcement agencies in this country, as well as certain military special operations personnel and other government agencies; all of the information on how to execute these maneuvers is open source and out there for any criminal, thug, terrorist, or other low life to find and master. Knowing how to counter these tactics is a prudent move for anyone who takes learning to be an evasive driver seriously. Now I am not going to give a tutorial on how to properly execute a P.I.T maneuver because I think we can all agree that some knucklehead is going to read this article and then go out and try it on the first person to look at him oddly; but I will say that the idea is to ram a vehicle on the side and rear and simultaneously accelerate, thereby putting your adversary into a spin as they run off the road. There is no way to stop this technique when it is executed properly. The best thing you can do if someone tries to P.I.T you is to keep your vehicle speed at under 35 mph and don't let the stress you are experiencing take control of the way you are driving; when cars fight, speed is never your friend. If you see someone coming up to align with one of your rear quarter panels, slow down or speed up a bit, as it will make it harder for your attacker to find the P.I.T "sweet spot" and should cause him to be stressed out and make a mistake. This will also buy you some time to get to a more populated area where an assailant would most likely break away from his attack to avoid detection.

Note: Speeds over 40 mph can be lethal, possibly causing the victim to lose control of the vehicle and flip.

WHAT TO DO IN THE EVENT OF CIVIL UNREST

Photo Credit: GettyImages

The best time to plan for an emergency is ahead of time, not when the emergency is happening. Always have a plan for what to do in the event of civil unrest. Keep embassy or consulate numbers on you at all time and make sure that if you are traveling to a country where civil unrest is common, give a copy of your itinerary to the embassy so that they will know of your whereabouts.

HAVE A PLAN OF WHERE TO GO

Always have a plan where to go and a fallback location in the event of an emergency such as civil unrest or riots and demonstrations. The embassy should be your first choice, but the airport or even your hotel room may work as long as you can get word to the embassy as to where you are. This is extremely important in the event that the embassy is going to conduct Noncombatant Evacuation Operations (NEO).

If you are in your hotel room, stay away from windows and keep your curtain drawn. Remember to stay alert and read your environment. At the first sight of civil unrest, you should call the embassy and let them know you are safe and what your location is or pay someone to deliver a message to the embassy. Avoid large crowds of people and do not advertise that you are an American, particularly if the unrest is aimed at the West. Even "peaceful" protests can quickly become violent riots. Try to stay in a safe place and behind thick walls to avoid small-arms fire and rocket-propelled grenades. Stay away from windows and doors. Be prepared to move to your preplanned location (such as the embassy) as soon as the opportunity arises. Another thing you can do to prepare for civil unrest is to always know exactly where your papers needed to exit the country are located. Keep a small backpack ready at all times with some cash (local and US), a credit card, rations, and water.

As I mentioned earlier in the book, the more you understand the history and current political and social climate before you travel, the better chances you will have of diverting your travel plans until the situation improves. The Internet is a great resource and you can find out a lot about a place by simply reading the news or going to a travel advisory website such as the one run by the State Department. While civil unrest cannot always be predicted, some places are clearly more volatile than others, so maintain your situational awareness at all times. If there are strong indicators of civil unrest, consider postponing your trip. If you are traveling to a country because of the civil unrest (such as a reporter or a member of the news media), know what you are getting into and act with extreme caution; one of the most dangerous situations travelers can find themselves in is a riot or an angry crowd where mob rules are in effect and people act in the collective, with no feeling of individual responsibility or empathy. The more you research and understand the environment you are entering, the safer you will be.

Professional criminals are predictable; but the world is full of amateurs.
Photo credit: GettyImages

4

Security and Safety on the Home Front

HOME SECURITY

Professional criminals are predictable. If they think you are home, or if they perceive your home to be a hardened target, they are not going to chance it; they will simply move on to a home that poses less of a threat. In a perfect world you could simply hang up a "Beware of Dog" sign and an ADT lawn post and then call it a day. The only problem is that while professional criminals are predictable, the world is full of amateurs. With Lord knows how many unstable, unintelligent, and unpredictable meth-heads, gang-bangers, and bottom feeders, and the whole host of other halfwits who are constantly contributing to the ever-rising violent crime and home intrusion rates in America today, your best bet in lowering your risk of becoming another statistic is to take a "holistic" approach to being as proactive as you can by taking measures to lower your chances of being victimized. But guess what? There is some good news. Contrary to what many security monitoring companies tell you in order to get you to sign into long, expensive contracts, you can actually take all the steps needed on your own to protect yourself and your property from these criminals. You don't have to spend thousands of dollars on hi-tech surveillance systems and long, costly security monitoring contracts in order to do it either. By keeping these three rules in mind, you will be taking your property's security into your own capable hands and you will send a message to criminal scum that they should keep on walking because your property is not a place they want to risk breaking into.

The majority of crimes in America go unsolved, and while a persistent police presence can be a deterrent to crime, the reality is that underfunding in the most crime-infested areas leaves the police with their hands tied. For all intents and purposes, they have become a reactionary organization at best. Let's face it, in our nation's most crime-ridden locations you will find a police force that is overworked, underpaid, and led by politicians who care more about votes than they do about cracking down on crime. Most of us don't want someone to take a report from us after we have been victimized. We want action to be taken to prevent the crime from happening in the first place or, at a minimum, to ensure that anyone who commits a crime against us will be caught, successfully prosecuted, and convicted. So, at the end of the day, if you want to protect yourself, your loved ones, and your property, you are just going to have to take measures to do it yourself, and that is the unfortunate reality of the society that we live in today.

CHOOSE YOUR NEIGHBORHOOD AND YOUR NEIGHBORS WISELY

If you are not in a situation where you can choose the area you want to live in, or if you already have a residence and you just want to fortify your property so that you are less of a soft target to criminals, there are still plenty of things you can do to that end. I will discuss them in detail as we move forward, but for now let's look at what to do if you are in the initial phases of trying to find a place to live.

While it is not always possible to have much of a choice as to the general area that you reside in, and where it is true that areas change, sometimes dramatically with the ebbs and flows of the economy, it does not change the fact that the most ideal way to set yourself up for success when it comes to securing your property is

Photo Credit: GettyImages

to choose an area to live in that has a strong economy and a large and thriving population of middle and upper class citizens, as these areas tend to have the best funded police, the lowest crime rates, and the most engaged populace when it comes to reporting and preventing criminal activity.

Once you have made the preliminary decision to live in a particular neighborhood, or if you already have a home or apartment in mind; before you sign onto a lease or purchase a home, be sure to spend a few hours on a Saturday night someplace in close proximity to where you are considering living, either by driving through the neighborhood or sitting in your car with the lights off, observing from a bit of a distance what type of human traffic and activity is prevalent. You would be shocked at how much an area can contrast from one time of day or day of the week to another. Another thing to be on the lookout for when searching for an area to live is the presence of Community Watch signs. A neighborhood that has an active Community Watch is a good sign that the residents of that community are proactive about keeping crime out and that they can be counted on to be part of the solution and not the problem.

If you want or need to live in an urban or suburban location, you will want to find a area that has a thriving economy, a large middle class, and a large population of young, educated professionals, as these types of areas enjoy the lowest overall crime rates. It is also very important to pay close attention to the physical characteristics of the property you are considering moving in to. In semi-urban and suburban areas, look for a house with a garage for off-street parking. If you are looking at condos or apartments, look at how well the grounds are kept. See if there is staff onsite and available 24/7 and check to see what kind of passive or aggressive security measures, such as surveillance cameras, doormen, and roving security, are integral to the facility. You can also take a look at the cars parked in the lots or garages, as they are a definite indicator as to the affluence of the residents. A gated community is an advantage if you are looking to reside in a suburban setting, but quite honestly they can also be a bit of a paper tiger if the criminals you are trying to protect yourself from live within the same gated community as you do. On the other hand, if your bank account can handle it, there are gated communities that go far beyond the simple presence of a gate with a pass code needed to lift it. If you have the money, you can find communities that offer both passive security in the form of security cameras that feed into CCTV, which is being monitored 24/7, as well as active security measures such as the use of gate guards with access rosters and a direct line of communication to the residents, static and roving armed security patrols, and many other security-minded amenities that help to mitigate the risk of crime. If you want to live on a larger piece of property, you are probably looking at living in a more rural community. The bottom line is, if you have the opportunity to choose the neighborhood you live in and the neighbors you live next to, choose wisely.

Whether you are looking to purchase a house, rent an apartment, or move into a trailer park, the primary consideration should always be location. When you are looking for a place to live, you probably have a general area in mind, based on your access to your job, or to your kid's school, or maybe even the hospital if you or a loved one suffers from a health issue. Starting with the town, village, or even county for those living in more rural areas, you can stop by the local police or sheriff's department and find out what kind of reputation for illegal activity, gangs, drugs, prostitution, or any other history of crime exists in the location you are looking at settling in. Residential areas are not always what they would appear to be; and crime infestations are not only a problem in urban environments. You may be surprised how many "quiet little towns" in rural America are actually cesspools of methamphetamines, crime, and disparity.

Rural communities are not always without problems of their own, contrary to popular belief. Many rural areas in America have been devastated by the ever-dwindling availability to jobs in agriculture and the movement of plants and factories to Mexico, China, and other foreign localities. The loss of jobs on such a large scale is known to bring drugs, crime, and disparity to many of America's rural communities, and that is why it is so important to do your due diligence in research before choosing where you are going to reside.

THERE IS STRENGTH IN NUMBERS

If you already live in a community that has a problem with criminal activity, there are plenty of things you can do to up your security posture, and with the help of neighbors and concerned citizens it won't take much to dramatically increase the community's overall security. You should always start by getting to know your neighbors. You will find that the greatest and most powerful tool that you can have to lower the risk of becoming a victim to crime is the concerned and observant eyes of your neighbors. It never ceases to amaze me how people can live next to someone for decades and still know nothing about them. Even if you or your neighbors are not the sociable types and just want to be left alone, you should at least make an attempt to maintain a cordial relationship and to exchange contact information as well as travel plans. There are

Photo Credit: GettyImages

plenty of other things you can do to bring people together when it comes to securing your home and community. You can join one of the local churches, temples, or other religious organizations, as they provide an excellent opportunity to network with other security-minded people within the community. Local gun clubs and firing ranges are another way to come together with other people within your community who are as dedicated as you are to making the area a safer place for everyone.

The more you know the people who live around you, the more effective your outer security ring is going to be. Sometimes people are afraid to initiate contact, but are motivated to help; they just don't have the social skills to make the first move. Don't isolate these kinds of people, insulate them. Make the first move and start the conversation going about coming together as a community to make it a safer place. If there is not a neighborhood watch, then contact the local law enforcement agency for assistance in getting one started yourself. You will be surprised how many people are willing to follow your lead but were just afraid to take the first step.

JUST BECAUSE YOU ARE PARANOID DOES NOT MEAN YOU ARE WRONG

Put your paranoia to good use by being proactive about your security by taking the steps to secure your home and property. Be suspicious of strangers, especially if they are asking personal questions about you and family members or neighbors. If work crews and utility companies are operating near your home, contact their respective company to verify the nature of their work and the personnel assigned to be at that site before letting them into your house or onto the property. Be cautious of salespeople, pollsters, and other strangers. If a suspicious vehicle is in the neighborhood, write down the license plate number and alert the police immediately. If something looks or sounds suspicious, do not be afraid to contact the police. When you are planning on being away from your home for more than a day or two, arrange to have your mail picked up and your trash can rolled back to your house away from the curb. When you travel away from your home in the winter, arrange to have your driveway plowed and ask a neighbor to make footprints going to and from your doors. In the summertime, arrange to have your yard mowed periodically so the grass never looks uncut. These are indicators criminals look for to determine if anyone is in your home. You can also go to just about any home improvement store and purchase a light timing system so that different lights throughout your house come on randomly at different times to give the appearance that someone is always home. Dogs are also an excellent "thief repellent," and it does not mean you need to own a German shepherd to get the job done. In fact, the sound or sight of any dog, regardless of breed or size, will greatly lower your risk of being robbed. If you can't or don't want to have a dog, you can go to any home improvement store or go online and find a motion-activated device that "barks" loudly, both randomly throughout the day, and whenever it senses movement. Criminals do not want to be detected by anyone. That is why the majority of home invasions happen between 1:00 p.m. and 2:30 p.m. when the majority of people are either at work or at school. Another thing criminals don't want to be is shot. So knowing that, you would think that a "Beware of Owner" sign showing the business end of a 44 Magnum would be a deterrent to getting broken into, when in fact the opposite is true. If you own guns, the last thing you want to do is advertise that fact to anyone, as word can get around and if the wrong people hear about it you may be targeted for theft specifically for the purpose of stealing your firearms. This is the reason why the majority of weapons used to commit crimes in the United States are stolen weapons. When in the home, lock the house up at night and secure the garage. If the house keys are lost or stolen or if moving into a previously owned residence, be sure to replace the locks immediately. Many cars have alarm switches on the key chain. Keeping them near you at night and activating them in the event of a suspected prowler or break-in will attract the neighbor's attention that something is wrong and may even scare off the intruder.

There are many other proactive steps you can take to reduce the threat of crime in your home and the surrounding neighborhood. You can start by cutting the shrubs around your home low to minimize places for prowlers to hide. If you are going out of town and your neighbor is unable to pick up your newspaper and retrieve your mail, ask to have these services stopped prior to leaving for an extended period. You can purchase a small safe from any big box store, sometimes for about a few hundred dollars. Be sure to find a remote and hidden location in your home to place the safe and then be sure to securely fasten the safe to the floor or wall so that a criminal can't just walk away with the entire thing. Try to always keep your most valuable smaller items in the safe when you don't have them in your possession. When you are going to be gone for any extended period of time, consider transferring your valuables from your safe to a safety deposit box at your bank. When you leave your home, avoid "hiding" keys outside, as some insurance policies will not pay if the break-in shows no signs of a forced entry. You can also ask the police, a trusted friend, or neighbor to check periodically on the residence.

You can get wireless window alarms, glass break alarms, door alarms, motion detectors, and infrared video cameras that are connected by the Internet directly to your smart phone. This allows you to instantly get an alert and you can watch a live video feed on your phone every time there is movement in or around your home.

One of the best deterrents to becoming burglarized is the presence of good 360-degree lighting. These days, lighting is cheap to buy and easy to install. I recommend that you put it all around your home and property and make sure you get lights with the option to either turn on manually or by the detection of motion. I also recommend you supplement the electrically powered lights with several strategically placed solar-powered spotlights so that you will have illumination in the event that the power goes out. Other steps you can take to fortify your home are to install a solid wood or metal-framed door that has, at a minimum, an unyielding deadbolt lock and security chain installed. A locksmith or a carpenter can install a more intricate locking security system than standard items from your local hardware retailer. Make sure the door has a one-way peephole. Remember to invest in good, secure side and rear doors as well. Sliding patio doors are notoriously easy to pick. You can override this fact by simply placing a 2x4 or pole down as a doorjamb when not in use, or you can buy a door jamb manufactured specifically for this purpose. Skylights should have bars with locks installed and ground floor windows and glass doors should have metal gratings with interior release mechanisms that are not accessible from the outside. All windows should have solid locking devices. Just about every home improvement store carries a plethora of security devices designed for the average Joe to install on his or her own.

HOME PROTECTION FIREARM SELECTION

Shotguns, assault style rifles, and pistols all make for a versatile home protection selection. Photo Credit: GettyImages

The importance of a firearm for home protection cannot be stressed enough. The only caveat is that you must seek proper training and be fully prepared to use the firearm when faced with danger. A firearm in the hands of a person who does not have this training or is unable to use it is extremely dangerous. You may obtain firearms training by joining a local shooting club or through most reputable gun shops. It is also imperative to understand all safety precautions and the firearm laws for the state in which you reside prior to acquiring a firearm.

ESTABLISHING A HOME DEFENSE PLAN

Regardless of whether you live in a large home on hundreds of acres of property deep in the country or in a tiny apartment in the city, it is imperative and vital that you establish a home defense plan to protect what is yours. From a tactical perspective you already have the advantage so far as you are on the defense and essentially static

Having fast and easy access to your home-defense weapon is essential if you actually want to be able to protect yourself and your loved ones from a home invasion. Obviously you will need to weigh the accessibility risk against the possibility that a family member or guest that is not trained and trusted in the use of firearms may get a hold of your weapons, so do what you need to in order to mitigate risk as far as you can. The bottom line is that if someone can get to you before you can get to your firearm then it's game over.

while the intruder or intruders are going to have to move in order to get to you and possibly expose themselves to your defensive fire in doing so. You can expand on this advantage by setting up "fighting positions" with prepositioned ammunition in select locations around your house and property. In order to make a home defense plan, you first need to identify the "fatal funnels," which are the most likely entry points into your home where an intruder can be expected to enter. Do not forget to take into consideration windows and any other openings that could possibly be breached by a determined intruder. The next step is to find points of domination, which are simply pre-planned fighting positions that provide excellent observation and fields of fire of the entire perimeter of your home and property. You should also identify potential entry points coupled with good cover and concealment. If you live in a multi-level dwelling, then you should determine a strong point at the highest level that you can, in order to provide yourself with a tactical advantage while still giving you the freedom of concealed movement to multiple vantage points around the circumference of the home. Finally, I cannot stress enough the importance of rehearsing your plan once you have devised it. Assess it and make adjustments in order to finalize your plan. Have the confidence of knowing that you have minimized the areas of "dead space" or places around your home where an intruder can approach, move, or hide without your seeing them.

SHOOTING THROUGH WALLS (OVER PENETRATION):

One thing you want to consider when shooting inside of your home is the chance of over penetration or shooting through walls and potentially harming an innocent person. The fact is that while shotguns are my preferred weapon

of choice for home defense, I could easily make an argument against them in favor of a pistol or a carbine such as an AR15. It is important to remember that weapons are tools and firefights are dynamic, meaning that it's good to have different available options so you can pick the right tool for the job. Pump shotguns make a distinct sound when racked, which could scare away an intruder, but on the other hand it could also expose your position. It also takes time to rack a round, which could be too late to react to an oncoming threat. Pistols are great, and hollow-point ammunition is preferred for knock-down power, but as counterintuitive as it seems a 9mm pistol round will penetrate much more wall material than a faster 5.56 (.223) round, which is designed to tumble on impact. So if over penetration is a concern, there is that consideration. Weapon placement and load status are also factors you need to consider when coming up with a home defense plan.

12-gauge Catamount Fury II shotgun from Century International Arms.

Note: You can mitigate the issue of having your pump shotgun giving away your position every time you rack in a round and increase your overall lethality by using a semi-automatic, magazine fed, blowback-operated shotgun such as the AA-12 Atchisson assault shotgun made by Sol Invictus Arms with Tactical Superiority, Inc. or the 12-gauge Catamount Fury II shotgun from Century International Arms. A semi-automatic pistol does not need to be racked/pumped and can be fired instantly once it has an initial round chambered, as opposed to a pump shotgun that needs to be racked every time you want to shoot a shell.

OTHER WAYS OF REDUCING THE THREAT OF CRIME IN YOUR HOME

If possible, do not put a name on the mailbox and cut shrubs low to minimize places for prowlers to hide. When not in the house, leave on some lights and a television. Use a set of timers to rotate different lights and televisions in order to turn on and off at different times. This will throw off anyone watching to ascertain if the house is a possible target. If a neighbor is unable to pick up the newspaper and retrieve the mail, ask to have these services stopped prior to leaving for an extended period. Put valuables in a safe in a hidden location. Avoid "hiding" keys outside and ask the police, a trusted friend, or neighbor to check periodically on the residence. When in the home, lock the house at night and secure the garage.

Identity theft is also something you should be aware of and take precautionary measures against. Shred unwanted mail and other personal documents and be cautious about what you place in garbage cans outside your house.

IDENTIFY SUSPICIOUS ACTIVITY

Join the neighborhood watch, if one exists, and get to know the neighbors. It always pays to have a friendly eye watching over your residence when away from home.

VETTING DOMESTIC EMPLOYEES

If planning to hire domestic employees, be sure to go through a reputable company that provides references and a full background investigation. You can also conduct an independent investigation using local police, neighbors, and friends. Provide employees with boundaries and establish off-limits areas right from the start.

Be careful how much sensitive information you provide to them. Never discuss travel plans or locations/times with anyone outside of your personal circle of trust.

So, remember, choose the neighborhood that you plan to settle in wisely, doing all of the due diligence to set yourself up for success by finding a place that is inherently one least likely to be broken into. Next it's time to get out there and make some friends! Don't forget that one of the most effective ways the police have of catching criminals red handed is when criminal activities are reported by concerned neighbors and residents. Finally, once you are in your home, don't forget to take every possible precaution within reason to harden your security posture and lower your chances of being robbed, or at least ensuring that if you are robbed that the culprits won't get away with their crime.

Understanding Terrorism and Reducing the Threat of Becoming a Terrorist Target

Have you ever wondered how someone became a "terrorist?" Is a terrorist a freedom fighter battling a numerically and technologically superior enemy with guerilla-like tactics? Or, is a terrorist a fanatical zealot, willing to kill anyone, even non-combatants such as women and children, because they believe that it will better their cause? Many definitions exist for both "terrorist" and "terrorism." In the United States, the word "terrorist" has become synonymous with any extremist group or individuals who have no regard for human life. The Federal Bureau of Investigation (FBI) defines terrorism as something that "involves violent acts or acts dangerous to human life; appears to be intended to intimidate or coerce a civilian population; to influence the policy of a government by intimidation or coercion; or to affect the conduct of a government by mass destruction, assassination, or kidnapping." Terrorism is a tactic that has existed since the beginning of warfare.

UNDERSTANDING THE THREAT

To better understand the terrorist threat in any given geographic location, some research is going to be necessary. The following questions are representative of the information you must have to maintain situational awareness.

- If traveling, are there terrorist groups in that designated area? Are those groups known to be violent?
- How active have they been?
- Do they normally target American citizens?
- Which techniques, tactics, and procedures do they employ?
- Are their actions predictable?
- What is their level of sophistication?

Additionally, it is also advisable to get an understanding of the demographics of the location you will be visiting and try to get a feel for whether or not the local citizenry is likely to warn or help you in a time of crisis. A Top Secret security clearance is not required to obtain this information. All you need to do is to conduct a simple search of the Central Intelligence Agency's (CIA) "The World Factbook" website or the United States Department of State Travel Advisory website.

- https://www.cia.gov
- https://travel.state.gov

TERRORIST METHODS

Recent terrorist attack methods have included vehicle bombs, letter bombs, skyjacked aircraft, chemical and biological weapons, improvised explosive devices (IEDs), assaults with small arms, kidnappings, murders, suicide bombers, assassinations, arson, and sabotage. Terrorists seek localities frequented by American and other foreign tourists, such as major shopping venues, discothèques, and hotels. They look for targets with specific characteristics, such as people who appear to be American or from the West, government officials, or persons of high stature and/or wealth. Oftentimes terrorists are opportunists, just looking and waiting for a "soft" target to focus in on.

HOW TERRORISTS TARGET PEOPLE AND INFRASTRUCTURE

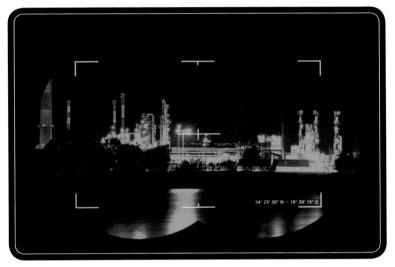

Photo Credit: GettyImages

In order to understand terrorist methods and targeting techniques, it is first important to be aware of the Terrorist Planning Cycle (TPC). You can find descriptions of the TPC in numerous Force Protection/Anti-terrorism (FP/AT) manuals and learning tools on the web, including the Department of Defense Anti-Terrorism Level I Training Program.

Understanding the TPC will build situational awareness to potential terrorist activity.

THE SEVEN PHASES OF THE TERRORIST PLANNING CYCLE

1. The first phase in the TPC is broad target selection. Broad target selection starts when terrorists collect data on various targets and make an evaluation of potential targets in terms

of public attention, their symbolic value, the level of critical infrastructure that would be affected, and the number of casualties that would likely be produced.

2. The second phase in the TPC is intelligence and surveillance. During this phase, targets identified in the first phase as being the most vulnerable, as well as meeting the other target criteria explained in that phase, are selected for additional in-depth intelligence collection and surveillance. This will determine guard patterns, patterns of life, and the physical layout of infrastructure. This phase may take days, weeks, or years, depending on the sophistication of the terrorists involved.

3. The third phase of the TPC is specific target selection. During this phase, terrorists choose a specific target for attack based on their outcome goals.

4. Phase four of the TPC is pre-attack surveillance and planning. During this phase, terrorists continue to have "eyes on" their objective target by conducting continuous surveillance. Additionally, during this phase, they initiate recruitment of other terrorists, or those with specialized skills needed by the organization to carry out their assault. It is during this phase that the terrorists will determine what the method of attack will be and where they will obtain the logistics (equipment, supplies, and explosives) to carry out the strike. If it is not a suicide attack, this is also the phase in which terrorists identify planned escape routes.

5. The fifth phase of the TPC is rehearsal. During this phase, terrorists conduct rehearsals or "dry runs," often at the actual site they plan to attack in order to test assumptions and to identify gaps and seams in their plan. It is also possible that, during this phase, the terrorists will facilitate an event at the site of the planned attack. Rehearsals are intended to test the reaction time of local authorities.

6. The sixth phase of the TPC is actions on the objective. This phase of the TPC consists of the actual planned attack

by the terrorists on their target. The factors in a terrorist's assessment of the best time to conduct an attack include identifying how to introduce the element of surprise, violence of action, and when the terrorist can cause the most damage to people and infrastructure.

7. The seventh and final phase of the TCP is escape and exploitation. Unless the attack is a suicide mission, this is the point where the terrorist attempts to flee through a planned escape route. This is also the phase where the terrorist organization that sponsored the attack would exploit its success by making recorded or pre-planned statements available to the news media or other organizations in order to promote their cause.

HOW TO REDUCE THE THREAT OF YOUR VEHICLE BEING TARGETED OR TAMPERED WITH

VEHICLE INSPECTION

You should always conduct a vehicle inspection before getting into the vehicle when driving in a country overseas, where you may be a target of terrorism, or whenever you suspect that others have tampered with the vehicle. Start with a visual inspection of the exterior of the vehicle. Try to identify if anyone tampered with the body, doors, undercarriage, or wheel wells of the vehicle. Look into the windows of the vehicle for evidence that someone has tampered with something on the interior. Leave something on your seat to see if someone moved it in order to tamper with your vehicle. If vehicle bombs are a threat, look for exposed wires under the seats or on the floor. Continue the inspection under the hood of the car and in the trunk, as well as through the entire interior. If you suspect that others have tampered with the vehicle, do not get in and do not turn on the ignition. Call the authorities and let them deal with the problem.

OTHER TIPS TO HELP ENSURE YOUR VEHICLE IS NOT TAMPERED WITH

Threats during ground travel can be a clear danger depending on where you are traveling. Here are some other tips you can take whether at home or abroad in order to mitigate risk while traveling in a vehicle:

- Do a thorough inspection of the interior and exterior of your vehicle each time prior to entry.
- Maintain situational awareness when getting out of the vehicle.
- Be aware of suspicious people or goings-on.
- When driving, be aware of criminal schemes like the "Bump & Rob," where the vehicle behind you hits your bumper and when the driver gets out of the car to check the damage, the passenger in the other vehicle gets behind the wheel in the victim's car and both cars drive away.
- To mitigate the risk of being carjacked in the first place, always drive with the vehicle windows up and the doors locked.

TERRORISM IN THE MAIL: HOW TO IDENTIFY SUSPICIOUS PACKAGES AND ENVELOPES

There is always the possibility of terrorists using the postal service to deliver damaging or lethal packages or substances such as were experienced with the Unabomber as well as the more recent Anthrax attacks. It is for this reason that having the knowledge to recognize when a package is suspicious is so important. It is important that you maintain your situational awareness of the following key indicators that the package or envelope that you receive may be a danger:

- The package looks lopsided or asymmetrical.
- Wires are protruding from package or an electronic device heard inside of package.

- There is no return address on package.
- An excessive amount of tape used to close the package.
- It is marked "Personal."
- There is an unknown odor resonating from the package.
- Powder is leaking out of the package.
- The package has oily stains on it.
- The writing on the package is misspelled.
- The package is not to an individual, but rather to a title only.
- Foreign postage or excessive postage is on the package.

Surviving Captivity: From Government Detention to Hostage Survival

Think of captivity in general as being that of governmental entities or non-governmental entities. As a rule of thumb, the closer the captor is to a governmental entity, the more you may expect decent treatment. Governmental entities normally follow some form of laws and regulations that regulate prisoner treatment. Hostage-takers are usually non-governmental in nature and therefore tend to be the hardest to predict as far as treatment is concerned. It is important that if you end up in a hostage situation, you use your situational awareness to determine the captor's motives.

WHAT TO DO IF ARRESTED OVERSEAS

MAINTAIN YOUR INNOCENCE

If detained by an overseas government entity, such as the police, you should always maintain your innocence. An admission of guilt could lead to fines, imprisonment, or worse, depending on

Photo Credit: GettyImages

the accusation. The legal protections provided by a foreign government may be greatly limited, compared to your rights in the United States.

US EMBASSY: ASK EARLY AND ASK OFTEN

Be very persistent in asking to speak to someone from the American embassy or consulate. If there is not a US Embassy in that country, ask to speak to someone from the "A, B, C" countries (Australia, Britain, Canada).

HOW TO CONDUCT YOURSELF WHILE BEING DETAINED

You must maintain bearing and courtesy at all times. Remember to control emotions and do not get into a conversation, interview, or interrogation with the police if detained on a serious charge. Be sure to ask the nature of your detention and be persistent until the detention authority provides an answer. Respectfully decline to talk and ask to speak to someone from the embassy as soon as it is evident that the offense is a serious one. American diplomatic personnel from the embassy can help provide an attorney who understands the laws of the detaining country.

Lesser offenses may be easier to talk your way out of or you may be able to pay a simple fine. Again, you must always use situational awareness. Do not initiate the offer of a bribe because it may lead to compounding potential legal offenses. Cooperate and be courteous and polite at all times. The police may just want to question your passport or other paperwork, ask about something in your bag, or simply try to eliminate a list of suspects from a larger investigation. Not every time the police question individuals is it for a serious matter. You should always ask if you are being placed under arrest. Stay alert and make sure to understand what is going on before talking to anyone. If detained, you usually have the right to know why. If language is an issue, demand an English-speaking attorney. Ultimately, if you are arrested and determine that an immediate release is not imminent, you must get word out to the American embassy. Embassy officials will be able to get word to family members, help with money transactions, ensure humane treatment, and help to facilitate legal representation.

SURVIVING A HOSTAGE SITUATION

Hostages are often forced to endure months and even years of complete isolation, which can be more damaging mentally than even physical torture. Because of this fact, psychologists who specialize in helping former hostages recover suggest doing whatever you can to keep your mind busy when isolated through imagination, meditation, making a schedule, exercising, or whatever else to keep your mind occupied. Photo Credit: GettyImages

One of the most dangerous moments of hostage captivity is the moment of capture—usually due to high levels of stress and adrenaline, both from the captors and the captives. Since the captors will almost always be armed, it's important to gain control of your emotions and not appear to resist. That said, the time of capture is often also the best time to escape due to the fog of war, so if you see an opportunity, then you must decide if the risk of capture outweighs the risk of attempting an escape; if so, then make a break for it. Photo Credit: GettyImages

Blindfolds may be used to disorient you or so that your captors are not seen by you. If used, be careful not to let them see you looking out under your blindfold as their not being recognized may be one of the factors keeping you alive. Photo Credit: GettyImages

When captured by a terrorist, it is probable that your captor will try and dehumanize you, as this makes the job of holding you captive or even torturing you much easier to do. To combat this, you should try to establish a one-on-one rapport with your captor by humanizing yourself through friendly conversation about topics common to both of you. Stay away from hot-button topics such as religion or politics, as it will only cause them to have their negative feelings towards you reinforced, which will put you in even more danger of being injured or killed. Photo Credit: GettyImages

Be aware of the Stockholm syndrome and don't fall victim to it while in captivity. Stockholm Syndrome normally occurs when a hostage becomes emotionally dependent on his or her captor and eventually begins to emphasize with the captor's struggle to a point where some have been known to switch over to the side of the terrorists who captured them. The syndrome got its name when Patty Hearst, granddaughter of William Randolph Hearst, a well-known American newspaper publisher, was kidnapped and eventually was arrested for partaking in an armed robbery as a member of the terrorist group that initially took her hostage. Photo Credit: GettyImages

Don't expect to eat well as a hostage. That said, it is very important to eat in order to maintain your strength and survive the situation, so this would be the time to get over any food aversions you may have and try to eat whatever they give you, no matter how unsavory or unappetizing it may look or smell. Photo Credit: GettyImages

You often hear the experts say that the use of torture as a means of extracting information is not effective and I would agree if it were not for the fact that just about everyone, including the United States of America, uses torture as a means of extracting information during interrogation. Whether it works well or not is anyone's guess, but regardless of its effectiveness I would say that you should be prepared to be tortured if you are ever unlucky enough to be taken hostage. My advice to you is to try to maintain your dignity the best you can. If they want information, then tell them anything. It doesn't even need to make any sense. The idea is to get them to stop long enough for you to regroup and bounce back. Don't beat yourself up for the things you may say under the duress of torture. There is no shame in it, as every person has a breaking point. Just don't let them break your will to survive. Photo Credit: GettyImages

A hostage situation is unlike any other captivity situation. Instead of being arrested by a recognized government entity for something that the captor feels was illegal, or being taken captive on a battlefield as a legitimate combatant, you are essentially kidnapped or taken against your will by a non-recognized, non-government entity. Additionally, the captors may have no intention of following or have no understanding of international law as it applies to the treatment of prisoners. In a hostage situation, your captors may be highly educated or they may have very little to no education at all. They may be highly organized professionals, or they may be a band of novices who are more afraid than you are. They could even be religious fanatics with no regard for the life of an "infidel" (nonbeliever). Hostage situations are a wild card. However, the chances of becoming a hostage are, for the most part, remote unless you are traveling in areas known for taking Westerners hostage, by groups such as the F.A.R.C in Colombia, pirates off the Somali coast, or in a war zone.

THREAT OF A SKYJACKING: TAKEN HOSTAGE IN THE AIR

Photo Credit: GettyImages

The attacks of 9/11 taught Americans and the world that terrorism poses a strong threat to those traveling by air. That said, the US Department of Homeland Security and global aviation security agencies have increased security precautions exponentially since then. Even with the increase in security safety measures, the threat of terrorism remains. This threat can increase significantly depending on where you travel around the world. You must remember situational awareness when traveling by air. If something looks suspicious, be sure to alert airport or airline officials immediately.

When traveling, there are certain situations of which you should be aware, including people who look nervous or out of place, baggage left unattended, and anything that looks out of place in an airport. While on the aircraft, you should look for people who seem suspicious, uneasy, or overly jumpy. 9/11 introduced a new tactic of using airliners as missiles to hit ground targets. Considering this, not every skyjacker is determined to commit suicide and some still have other motives for taking over an aircraft. That is why it is important for you to look at the situation and then decide whether to resist or cooperate.

SKYJACKING FACTORS FOR CONSIDERATION

In the event of traveling on an airplane that is the being skyjacked, there are certain factors that you should consider:

- First and foremost, did the perpetrators replace the flight crew with their own pilot or pilots? If they left the aircrew intact, this is a possible indicator that at some point they want the aircraft to land safely.
- Next, are they abusing passengers? This will give you a good idea of the hijacker's mindset.
- Finally, you can determine the goals of the hijackers by what they are doing.
- Are they telling everyone to stay calm? This may be an indicator that the use of the aircraft itself is the goal.

- Are they singling people out by nationality, race, religion, government affiliation, etc.? This can give insight into the hijacker's intentions and goals. The hijackers may announce that they have taken over the plane or it may come from the crew. Stay calm. Hijackings normally occur within thirty minutes to an hour after takeoff because the plane will have enough fuel to make it to the hijacker's chosen destination.

WHAT TO DO IF YOU ARE BEING SKYJACKED

You should return to or stay in your seat as soon as it becomes apparent that there is a situation. A discharged weapon could cause a decrease in cabin pressure and you may need the oxygen mask located at your seat. If you have a government affiliation, hide your papers and documents in a seat or in a magazine in front of you in the seat pocket. Use a tourist passport, if possible, when asked for passports. The most

Photo Credit: GettyImages

important thing to do is stay calm and try to determine what the captors' intentions are.

Prior to 9/11, the standard operating procedure was to cooperate with hijackers, but now the world has changed dramatically. Airline passengers are going to have to communicate with one another and make a decision whether to act aggressively toward the hijackers. It is suspected that this was the case on Flight 93, where the actions of forty passengers and crew may have thwarted the

9/11 hijackers from crashing the aircraft into the US Capitol. Use situational awareness, pay attention to the indicators mentioned above, and then act accordingly.

SURVIVING A LONG-TERM HOSTAGE CAPTIVITY SCENARIO

Photo Credit: GettyImages

Surviving a captivity situation, particularly one that is long term, will most likely be one of the most trying and difficult experiences you will ever have to endure. It is important that you never give up hope that you will be freed from your situation and be able to return home safely to your loved ones. Your inner strength and resilience will be the biggest factor in your survival and your greatest asset in your survival tool box.

WHAT TO DO AT THE TIME OF CAPTURE

Photo Credit: GettyImages

Photo Credit: GettyImages

The most dangerous time in any captivity situation is at first capture. This is the time when tensions are usually at the highest and the captor is most likely to use deadly force. Stay calm, be respectful, and maintain situational awareness. The point of capture is also one of the best times to escape, but you must be smart and understand when the best chance of survival will arise. Appear to cooperate with the captor's demands, particularly in the face of deadly force. In some hostage situations, you may realize that the captor does not see the captive as human at all, but rather as a symbol (money, politics, religion, or any number of issues) for whatever their motivation was for taking the hostage in the first place.

HUMANIZING YOURSELF AND ESTABLISHING RAPPORT

This can be a very dangerous situation, particularly if a person is being held by an extremist group like Al-Qaeda or other groups known for executing hostages. The best thing hostages can do is to humanize themselves by establishing rapport with the captor. Always remain cognizant of the possibility of Stockholm Syndrome. This occurs when a captive begins to feel so much empathy for the captor that he or she begins to side with the cause of the captor, as in the case of Patricia Hearst. The key for a captive is to get the captor to see the captive as a human being. You can do this by being friendly and talking about non-inflammatory subjects like missing family, sports, or any number of things. Stay away from hot-button topics like politics and religion. Gauge the captor's responses and if something seems like a sensitive subject, back away and talk about something else. Do not give up; it could take days, weeks, or even months or longer to establish rapport. In a hostage situation, doing this may save your life.

TREATMENT AS A HOSTAGE

Remember, it is difficult to predict the standard of living and treatment you may encounter as a hostage. Be prepared for physical abuse and unsanitary conditions. Expect sleep, food, and water deprivation. Through all of this, it is important that you maintain your personal dignity. Keep faith in the fact that the US government will be doing everything in its power, from diplomatic solutions to surgical strike operations, in order to set you free.

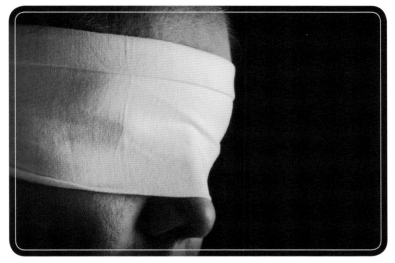

Photo Credit: GettyImages

EXERCISE YOUR MIND

Try to remember everything seen, heard, smelled, and touched while in captivity. Notice the different languages that are heard, what the captors are wearing, and everything you can about the locations in which you are held. All of this information can help

Photo Credit: GettyImages

develop your situational awareness, as well as prove useful for an escape or rescue. The key is to maintain some level of control, even if it is just being aware of your surroundings. While in captivity, it is imperative to do everything possible to maintain your health. Start an exercise regimen and do anything to keep the mind busy. For example, an American prisoner of war in Vietnam built a house in his mind, one brick at a time. Additionally, you should set routines to occupy time. Be prepared for a rescue at all times. Stay low to the floor in the case of a rescue attempt. If you hear bullets during the rescue attempt, stay in a low crouch; bullets tend to hug the floor and you have less chance of being hit by a bullet by staying off the ground. If grenades are going off, lie flat. Explosions tend to go upwards and you can minimize exposure to the explosion by staying low. You must always keep your hands where rescuers can see them. Do not pose a threat and wait for commands from rescuers.

HOW TO EXERCISE ESCAPE MINDEDNESS: KNOWING HOW AND WHEN TO TRY AND GET AWAY

Photo Credit: GettyImages

HOW TO PLAN AN ESCAPE

While this is in no way a book on how to circumvent security systems or holding facilities, and I am not going to go into any details on defeating constraints, I will tell you that there is literally a plethora of information out there for you to learn to do these things on your own without my help; simply do a Google search and find out what I mean for yourself. I choose not to discuss these things because with my background and the fact that it was once my job to teach these techniques, tactics, and procedures (TTP's) to US Special Operations Forces, I choose not to reinforce the fact that specific techniques have been taught to operators who today are out there defending our country, in harm's way, and always vulnerable to the possibility of being captured themselves. When you do your search, you may find that others do not feel as strongly about not advertising such trade craft, so I am certain you will find the information you seek even if it is without my assistance in doing so. That being said, I do want to talk about a few general topics about the state of mind one needs to be in to make an escape attempt, as well as a few of the more general and non-specific and non-TTP related steps that one can take to aid them in an escape attempt.

ESCAPE MINDEDNESS

An Afghan journalist was held captive by the Taliban for more than seven months along with his colleague, an American *New York Times* reporter, until they were able to plan and execute a daring nighttime escape that included weeks of careful plotting, taking advantage of weary guards, and dropping down a twenty-foot wall with a rope. The Afghan journalist said that the early morning escape from the second floor of a Taliban compound in Pakistan's northern tribal areas was a desperate attempt by two severely demoralized reporters who believed that the Taliban were not seriously negotiating and would hold them indefinitely or even possibly execute them in order to bolster recruitment and create propaganda. The two journalists along with their driver were abducted outside Kabul as they traveled to interview a Taliban commander for a book he was writing about Afghanistan. The three men were abducted on a road just a few minutes from where they planned to meet the Taliban commander, in the southeast of Kabul. One of the journalists had previously escorted two other foreign journalists to safe interviews with the commander, and during those meetings he made the mistake of assuming that the two had established a degree of trust. The journalists reported that once captured they were moved along with their driver multiple times by their captors to different safe houses until settling in their final location in the northern tribal area. The two men testified that they had been repeatedly threatened with death by their Taliban captors. The three months they spent in captivity were so "hopeless" that one of the men said that he considered committing suicide with a knife. As their captivity dragged on, the two men began plotting their escape by surveying the compound and its surroundings. One of the men stated that he faked illness to visit a doctor outside the complex. Other times he asked his captors if he could watch local cricket matches — a sport he pretended to adore—so that he could study potential escape routes. Still, it seemed impossible to escape from a town controlled by Taliban and foreign militants. The reporters were smart enough to realize that they needed to humanize themselves to their captors and establish some level of rapport if they were going to get them to become comfortable enough with them to let down their guard enough to create a window of opportunity for them to escape. One Friday evening, in a planned bid to keep their captors awake as late as possible to ensure that the men would eventually sleep soundly, one of the journalists challenged the militants who slept beside them in the same room to a local board game. When the games finally ended at midnight, the journalists waited for the militants to fall asleep. At 1 a.m., the journalists snuck out of the room. They made their way to the second floor, and got to the top of a five-foot-high wall. When they looked down, they said they were greeted by an unnerving view: a twenty-foot drop. Using a rope that one of the men had found and hidden two weeks earlier, they fastened the rope to the wall, and the first man lowered himself along the rope before unclenching his fists for good. He crashed to the ground, leaving him with a sprained right foot and other injuries. He cut his foot, he said, pointing to his swollen and heavily bruised ankle and his bandaged big toe. The second journalist then lowered himself along the wall and jumped down without injury. When asked why their captives did not hear the thump of their impact with the ground, the men stated that they waited to make the escape attempt on a night when the city had electrical power. At night, an old, noisy air-conditioner that ran masked the sound. As the two men walked away, dogs barked at them from nearby compounds. At one point, barking stray dogs rushed at them in the darkness. To their surprise, no Taliban members emerged from nearby houses. After walking for fifteen minutes, they arrived at a Pakistani militia post that one of them had spotted during one of his daytime trips outside the house. In the darkness, a half-dozen guards who suspected they were suicide bombers aimed rifles at them and shouted for them to raise their hands and not move. The men said that they were warned by the guards, "If you move, we are going to shoot you." As the two men stood shivering in the darkness, it took the Afghan journalist fifteen minutes of anxious conversation to convince the guards that he had been kidnapped along with an American journalist—who hardly looked the part, with his long beard and Islamic attire. The men were eventually allowed in the compound, ordered to take off their shirts, searched, blindfolded, and taken to the base's headquarters. After Pakistani officials confirmed their identities, they were treated well. Later that day, they were transferred to Islamabad, Pakistan's capital, and to an American military base outside Kabul. When asked about the status of the Afghan driver who had been captured and held captive with them, the journalists stated that the entire ordeal seemed too much for the man to handle emotionally and he appeared to stay in a constant state of being overwhelmed by fear of his captors and had therefore not participated in the planning or the escape.

The reason I am telling this story is because I believe it to be an outstanding example of how two men instinctively, and without any formal training, showed a high level of "escape mindedness" throughout the ordeal. They were able to not only spend weeks plotting and planning for an escape, but also had the sense to realize the need to establish one-sided rapport with their captors in order to create an environment most advantageous to making an escape attempt. It also shows how instead of succumbing to their predicament and allowing the severity of their situation to overwhelm them, the men were brave and daring enough to try to survive at all costs. They chose to fight a battle of wills against their captors that led them out the other end of their captivity experience triumphant because of it.

HOW TO ESCAPE FROM THE TRUNK OF A CAR

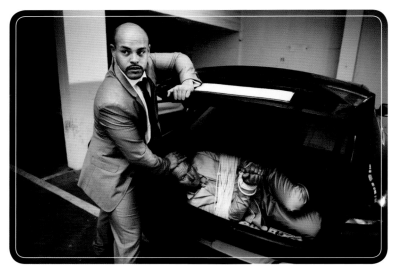

Photo Credit: GettyImages

You never know what type of situation you may find yourself in when you make the decision to make a break for it. One common place that abductors have been known to place hostages during their initial abduction or when being moved from one location to another is the trunk of a car. Being trapped in the trunk of a car by an abductor is a bad situation that can be deadly depending on the temperature outside and the oxygen and carbon dioxide levels in the trunk. It is important that you make every effort to escape. Here are some ideas of things you can do to aid in your getaway:

- US cars built since 2002 all have a trunk release cable running into the inner locking mechanism. If your abductors were careless enough to overlook this fact, pull the release cable and make your escape.
- If there is no cable release, you may be able to pry the latch open. Look under the rug for the jack lever and use it to pry the latch open.
- You can try to use the jack to open the trunk by jacking it up from the inside.
- If unable to get out from the trunk, try kicking out the brake lights and then sticking your hand out of the hole to signal other motorists that you have been abducted. Hopefully they will alert the authorities.
- Another technique you can try is to escape through the back seat if the kidnappers leave the car with you in the trunk. Try to use leverage and push or kick the back seat cushion out. Remember to stay calm. Most trunks are not airtight and you should still be able to breathe, although depending on the temperature outside the heat may be a factor. It is important that you keep your wits, don't panic, and breathe if you want to increase your chances of escape.

HOW TO JUMP FROM A MOVING VEHICLE

Jumping from a moving vehicle is extremely dangerous and should only be attempted in a life-threatening situation where the possibility of escape outweighs the injuries you may obtain by jumping.

- Try to slow the vehicle down by pulling the hand break if it is accessible.

- Plan your exit. Look for a spot where there is grass, mud, or soft dirt for you to land on. Make sure there are no obstacles that you will slam into once you jump.
- Open the door and push yourself out and away from the direction of the vehicle. Make sure you are facing the direction of travel when you jump.
- Keeping your hands in a position tight to your body protecting your head, try to simulate a parachute landing fall by collapsing your body to the ground starting with the balls of the feet and then rolling into the calves, thighs, buttocks, and your push-up muscle (the side of your upper torso). You want to keep your body in a tight position and roll; do not belly flop into the ground.
- If you survived the jump without injuries that would prevent you from getting up, then waste no time. Get up and move out swiftly, trying to put as much distance between yourself and your abductors as possible.

Note: This is an extremely dangerous maneuver and you could be seriously injured or killed in the process. Make sure you do a thorough risk analysis in your head before attempting this. If the risks associated with not jumping do not outweigh the risks of jumping, do not do it.

WHAT TO DO ONCE YOU HAVE COMMITTED TO AN ESCAPE

Once you have committed to escape, do not look back. Run to safety immediately. Since "safety" is a relative term that is totally dependent on where you are, there is no single answer on where to go. Normally, running into a crowd of people or to a police officer would be considered sufficient enough to make your pursuers give up. If, however, you are in a semi-permissive or non-permissive environment such as a war zone, you may have to run to a friendly patrol or to the US embassy to be considered truly safe.

Note: If you run to safety, understanding the culture of the people in the nation you are visiting is so important. Knowing basic phrases in the local language could mean the difference between life and death. A good example of this is Pashtunwali, the code of the largest ethnic group living in Afghanistan that mandates that if a stranger asks for help, it must be given.

WHAT TO DO IF YOU ARE ESCAPING OR EVADING AND YOU ARE BEING CHASED BY A TRACKING DOG TEAM

There are generally two main types of tracking dogs: those that use the air to track your scent and those that track your scent on the ground. Regardless, a good tracking dog is hard to defeat once they are onto your scent. Their biggest limitation is generally only that of the ability of the handler to keep up with them. It is a misnomer that you can simply enter the water to lose a dog team tracking you. The fact is that doing so can actually make your scent even stronger to them if the body of water is small and slow moving. If you want to use water to help you, then your best bet is to either jump into a fast-moving river with a flotation device such as something you fabricate or even a large branch of driftwood and then put as much distance between yourself and your trackers as you can before you touch land again. You can also swim into a large body of water toward the center and then button hook to a random angle on the shore. Other ways to throw off dogs are putting chemicals on the ground or even using pepper to cover your trail. That said, if the team is good, they will be trained to avoid such tricks. The bottom line is that if you are being chased by a professional dog team, it's a worst case scenario, and while you will most likely not be able to get them off your trail, you may be able to delay them long enough so you can get away. Here are a few tips to help you defeat or at least delay a dog tracking team and trackers in general:

1. Even the most highly trained tracking dogs can lose focus and become distracted. This will become a factor as the dogs become hungry and fatigued as the search develops. You can

assist this process by crossing difficult terrain and putting as much distance between yourself and the tracker team as you can in order to exhaust the dogs, which will make them more prone to losing focus and drive.

2. Scent plumes can vary greatly depending on the temperature, terrain, and weather conditions. The best time to lose a dog that is tracking you is on rocky uneven terrain when the sun is at its hottest. It will also help if there is little to no humidity to hold your scent plume.

3. Another thing you can do is to retard your scent. When I was in Afghanistan we used different chemicals to hide our scent when on sensitive sniper or reconnaissance missions. Some of these products are now available commercially. I'm not saying that they will make you invisible to a good K9 tracking dog, but they will definitely make your trail harder to pick up and follow.

4. The absolute best way to defeat a tracker, K9 and man alike, is to get in a car and drive away. This should be your number one objective if you are being tracked by a determined tracker or tracking team.

5. Don't leave articles of clothing or even soiled toilet paper or used tampons or bandages in a place that a tracking dog can use it to program in your scent. If the dog doesn't know what you smell like and they start searching for you in an area highly trafficked by other humans, then it is unlikely they will be able to pick up your scent or tracks, if it's a human tracker chasing you.

Going Off the Grid: How to Disappear and Not Be Found

Photo Credit: GettyImages

You often hear people saying they are going to "disappear," "lay low," or even "fall off the grid" so that no one will be able to find them. Believe me, as a retired special forces soldier I know I have made my fair share of enemies around the world, and because of that I have spent more than just a little time thinking of ways to stay off the radar. I can tell you that if someone is determined to find you in today's technologically advanced world, and they have the tools and knowledge to back them up, staying "unfound" is no easy feat. That said, it is not impossible. If you have the discipline and resources to do it the way I tell you to, you just might pull it off!

If your reason for bugging out is more complex than a SHTF scenario and your intent is to basically disappear and not be found in order to assure your personal survival, then you should try to buy yourself some time and stack the deck in your favor. If, for instance, you are running from an individual, group, or organization, then I will start by saying that to do it right, disappearing off the grid will take time and extreme discipline. If possible, you would need to slowly distance yourself from everyone in your life—friends, associates, family, even pets—until there is no expectation on anyone's part that you are going to try to contact them any time soon; this will help mitigate the chances of anyone coming to look for you or to contact you through the people in your life. Now if I were bugging out because some person or people were looking for me, then there are certainly some additional actions I would take. The first thing I would do is pull the proverbial plug. What do I mean by that? I would close all of my social media accounts and disconnect every single piece of electronics that I owned to remove any source of power to those items. Generally speaking, on the higher end of the spectrum only the government, the military, law enforcement, and foreign government agencies or entities will have access to the technology to find you from any sort of electrical or electronic signature that you may be unknowingly emitting. That said, on the lower end of the spectrum, anyone can get onto Facebook or check to see where a phone call originated from. As a rule of thumb, the more you are "linked in," the more chances there are that you will be found through the use of technology.

If you think someone may be trying to actively find you and you don't want them to, then you will need to take a few other things into consideration. If you have a later model vehicle, then you may not even know that it has certain theft and or emergency alert hardware that allows it to send a signal out, giving your exact location and in some cases even the ability to talk or listen to you theoretically without your even knowing about it. If you don't know how to disable or remove that hardware and you know or suspect that the person or people looking for you have the resources to tap into this type of technology, then I would suggest you leave the 2018 loaded SUV behind and get used to cranking down your window with a handle. One other caveat would be to make sure your vehicle is in good running condition, all the lights and other things that make it street legal are 100 percent and, if practical, travel with enough fuel to get you to where you are going so as to minimize stops and to mitigate the risk of being pulled over. Also remember to use back roads, as main roads often have cameras at toll stops and overpasses that will record your license plate number. Another thing to remember if you're trying to bug out and don't want to be found is public transportation. When it comes to choosing to use public transportation when you bug out, it really depends on why you are bugging out and who is looking for you. If you are bugging out because you are trying to get away from an abusive ex or something like that, and as long as the government is not actively looking for you, then I highly suggest you use public transportation. It is much harder to leave a trail for the average person to follow when traveling on a bus. The situation and the advice would be different in other cases and it all depends on the level of technological capabilities and assets possessed by the person or people who are trying to find you.

Now if you think someone is looking for you and your desire is to not be found, then the location you choose to bug out to can't belong to you or be associated with your. Avoid using a friend's property, since anyone who is aggressively trying to find you would surely follow that rabbit trail. I would suggest state or government forest/protected land, as it is the best way to hide right underneath someone's nose, but you have to go deep in and leave a low signature. Beware of park rangers and making any contact with anyone, as human contact outside of the person or group you are with (if you're not alone) is your weak link when it comes to not being found. The bottom line is that if you own an off-grid location or if someone you know owns the property, then it can lead a persistent pursuer to find you. All of that being said, not everyone is skilled enough or even willing to live alone in the wilderness, so if you plan to travel to an undisclosed location and continue to live within the confines of some sort of community or society, then you will at a minimum want to do the best job you can at disguising your appearance. Stay away from anything that requires you to use your real name. I would also suggest you stay away from credit cards and stick to cash to make your purchases. In addition to all of that, you can use prepaid cell phones, but remember that someone could still trace you back to the closest cell tower from where you made your calls. You may want to use a trusted intermediary to be the go-between to transmit and receive information so that nobody ever has a direct link to your location; particularly if those looking for you are persistent and savvy in their search for your whereabouts. I'm not going to go into any more detail on changing your identity in this book, but if you want to learn more you can read the work that I and others have written on the topic in other books, as well as online.

OTHER DO'S AND DON'TS WHEN YOU WANT TO DISAPPEAR AND NOT BE FOUND

Keep your mouth shut! Three people can keep a secret if two of them are dead, so try to limit who knows where you are going to the absolute minimum. Even then, unless they are actually to meet with you there, don't tell anybody where you are going or what's your plan is.

Cash is King! Slowly withdraw all of your bank accounts until they are empty and then close them one by one. You need to understand that part of not being found is that it is safest to be a cash-only type of person from that day forward. That means that if you are retired and receive a pension, if you get settlement money, child support, or an inheritance, none of those funds can be withdrawn if it is your intent not to be found, especially if the person looking for you has the knowledge and placement to access your financial transaction information. If you have no choice but to get money from your bank, then, in order to minimize the chance of future sightings, you should attempt to take out as much money as you are able to get in small bills. This is one of the reasons that going off the grid and disappearing is so difficult to do these days and why making such a decision is such a catastrophic event. In many cases the amount of time a person is capable of staying off the grid is directly proportional to the amount of cash he is able to get in his possession.

Stay away from debit and credit cards. Every time you use an ATM machine or you go into a store and buy something, you leave a video and electronic signature that you were there, allowing whomever may be searching for you with a virtual road map of your direction of travel and your last known location. That's why your best bet is to pre-plan as much and as far in advance as is humanly

Drones like this Raven-B that is being flown by one of the author's teammates after a firefight were often used by SF soldiers to get a Battle Damage Assessment (BDA) during lulls in fighting.

possible. You want to purchase your gear from multiple locations and with cash. Spread those purchases out over weeks or months if feasible. If money is going to be needed where you are going, then take cash with you. Again, time can only help you in this case, because if you purchase the gear you need slowly over time, you won't leave as bold of a signature than if you spend $5000 in one trip to REI.

BE AWARE: "BIG BROTHER" MAY BE WATCHING

If you are bugging out from a technologically superior adversary, then you should be aware of the fact that street cameras and store cameras are literally everywhere nowadays. Facial recognition technology has come a very long way since it was first introduced and the number of locations that are covered by cameras that are recording live video by both public and private entities has increased greatly. It is close to impossible to walk or drive anyplace in many of the more populated places in the US without being recorded, and any recorded video can be interrogated by facial recognition software. If you suspect that the person looking for you could have the knowledge and placement to tap into those systems, then your best bet is to either stay out of public completely or, if that is not an option, then consider distorting your appearance so that it will be difficult to recognize your key facial features such as eyes, nose, chin, and ears in the event that the your facial image is captured on video.

TECHNOLOGY IS A DOUBLE-EDGED SWORD

While watches, smart phones, computers, and other "smart" technology does a great job of helping to keep you in contact with friends and family and perform a plethora of other functions, from telling time and accessing weather data to staying in shape, they also often have GPS technology that can alert anyone who is looking for you as to where you are and where you have been. I am not saying to throw away your iPhone or laptop, I am just saying that if you don't have an in-depth knowledge of the technology that you possess to a point where you feel secure that your devices will not inadvertently give away your location to those seeking to find, then you must either counter the capabilities of those looking for you or don't take the chance with any device that has a GPS, beacon, radio signal, IP address, or any other function that could ping your location out into the atmosphere.

A PICTURE SAYS A THOUSAND WORDS

You need to consider the five W's when it comes to photographs: who, what, where, when, and why. If you don't want someone who may be searching for you to know any of the W's, then you need to try to eliminate any traces that such a picture ever existed. When you bug out, just know that if someone is looking for you, they can get a ton of information just by looking at photos you left behind, and that they could be used as powerful tools in trying to determine your current location. Because of this, it is smart to destroy all your hard copy photos that you don't take with you and to delete any photos you currently have posted online. Of course, it should go without saying that once you bug out you want to stay away from having your picture taken to the best of your ability.

WHAT TO DO ABOUT IDENTIFICATION

If you are trying to disappear, there are pros and cons to whether or not you should keep all of your identifying documents and ID cards or if you should destroy them. One thing for certain is that you should never leave those papers behind. If your plan is to create a new identity, then you may want to keep those documents to assist you in the process, but changing your identity is a completely different and separate class of instruction, so I'll save it for another book. Bottom line is that all of those documents contain clues that can help lead a pursuer to your location, so you need to take measures to ensure they never get that opportunity.

To sum it up, if you really want to fall off the grid and not be found, your first step should be to disconnect yourself from all electronic gadgets and tools like laptops, cell phones, and debit or credit card charges, and try to avoid being filmed by ATMs, street cameras, and other surveillance systems. At this point you have a choice to either travel deep into the wilderness and live off the land, leaving as low of a signature as possible, or, if living off the land is not your thing or you simply do not possess the skills to do so successfully (as most people do not), you need to find someplace to live where you can pay cash to live and buy all of the things you need to live with a cash-only rule. Remember to always take steps to disguise or distort your appearance in any way that you can. Between wigs, clothing, make up, prosthetics, and a few other creative props, you can do a decent job of this without spending a fortune. As you can see, there is a lot more that goes into bugging out and falling off the grid when your survival depends on not being found than most people have or ever will take into consideration.

8

Bugging In/Bugging Out: Know What You Need if You Intend to Stay, and When, Where, and How to Go When It's Time to Bug Out

One thing I spent a whole lot of time doing while serving in the Special Forces was coming up with ways to mitigate or "lower" risks by intricately planning and rehearsing for contingencies of what I would do "if." When it comes to bugging out, there are many possible scenarios or "ifs" to plan and rehearse for. I like to plan and rehearse for the absolute worst case scenario, since it normally will cover all of the essential moving parts (or "sub-tasks") of any of the lesser possibilities.

Now let's explore a few reasons why anyone would want to bug out in the first place. I mean, modern society has its perks, right? Well, one reason would be if the power grid and all that comes with it ceases to exist, then you won't have a choice but live a survival existence. But what would make you want to go off

Photo Credit: GettyImages

the grid intentionally? It could be any number of things: suppose you are a homesteader and your property's defensive perimeter has been breached and you are being overrun by hordes of outlaw biker gangs, or maybe an invading army is rolling tanks through your field. It could be because of internal fighting and civil unrest, rioting and anarchy, governmental collapse, or maybe you are running from a person or an organized criminal group. You may even be someplace where a government entity abroad is trying to track you down. The possibilities are endless, but the actions you should take don't really differ very much other than two basic factors: You are either running from a large population center because for whatever reason the proverbial shit has hit the fan and you need to get to someplace where you can find relative safety and the resources needed to stay alive, or you are bugging out because you feel personally threatened by a person, group, or organization and you to need to bug out to a safer and more secure location.

WHEN TO BUG OUT AND WHEN TO STAY IN PLACE

If you live in an urban or built-up area and any one of many catastrophic scenarios were to take place, then it would be in your best interests to bug out and get to a place that is as far from a major population center as possible. In a catastrophe, such areas will become dangerous as thousands, hundreds of thousands, or even millions of people will all be fighting for the same dwindling resources. These high population areas will see extremely high levels of social unrest, rioting, unchallenged crime, looting, and a plethora of other problems.

CONSTRUCT AN EDC (EVERY DAY CARRY) KIT: IN YOUR GREATEST TIME OF NEED, YOU WILL ONLY HAVE WHAT YOU HAVE

An EDC is nothing more than a group of items that you keep on your person or within arm's reach at all times. Hopefully you will never be so far from your Get-Back-Home Bag (GBH) or your Bug-Out Bag (BOB) that you won't have it when you need, it but Murphy's Law says that when disaster strikes you may only have what you are carrying on your person until you can make it to your BOB. This is why it is so important to come up with a feasible EDC so that you will never be left unprepared.

Every Day Carry (EDC)
- Concealed-carry pistol with additional magazine (refer to state law for permit requirements)
- Keys with lanyard
- Less-than-lethal device, key chain size (taser, stun gun, or mace)
- Survival kit, individual (key chain size)
- Flashlight, tactical, (key chain size)
- Multi tool with knife, key chain size (credit card knife if you need a lighter load/more discreet)
- Watch (smart watch technology)
- Cell phone (with charger cable, plug, spare battery pack)
- Install Survival Apps on cell phone (such as walkie-talkie app, first aid and CPR, GPS, and compass)
- Wallet with $200 cash (small bills) and credit/debit card

- Medical mask (folded in wallet)
- Paracord bracelet
- Tactical pen
- Wedding ring/gold ring (or other gold jewelry) for emergency barter

CONSTRUCT A GET-BACK-HOME BAG (GBH)

Not a bug-out bag; smaller and only geared towards getting you to your home from wherever you are when the SHTF.

GBH Contents:

- Food (one meal and several energy bars)
- Water (two quarts)
- Pry bar
- Bolt cutters
- Knife (full tang)
- IFAK (first-aid kit)
- Space blanket
- Mask (medical)
- Mask (chemical)
- Flashlight (headlamp style)
- Police Scanner, small
- AM/FM Radio, small
- Walking shoes
- Change of clothing (outdoor/ rugged)
- Rain poncho
- Sunglasses
- Goggles
- Glass/window punch
- Bandanna
- Charging devices (battery and solar)
- Crime prevention tools (mace, taser, baton)
- Paper map (local/detailed and large scale, showing clear routes back to your home)

Photo Credit: GettyImages

- GPS device
- Personal locator beacon/EPIRB
- Satellite phone and accessories

BUGGING IN: WHAT TO PLAN FOR IF YOU INTEND TO RIDE IT OUT FROM THE HOMESTEAD

While preppers and emergency preparedness folks (including myself) tend to talk a great deal about the concept of "bugging out," the fact is that if you live in a relatively safe and secure location and you have the resources to survive through a prolonged or even indefinite period of time without any resupply of essential goods, then it is actually advisable to remain in your home after a catastrophe or mass emergency scenario occurs. If you live in or near a city or other large population center, you need to be forewarned that such locations are literally powder kegs that can erupt in an instant in the event that the flow of essential supplies ceases to provide life-essential inventory such as food, water and medicine. The fact is that thousands if not millions of people will begin to fight for

Photo Credit: GettyImages

the dwindling resources that still exist. You can be certain that the human condition can be ruthless in times of desperation, and as peoples' survival instincts kick in, they can be expected to do almost anything to get what they need to survive. If you decide to remain in your home and you are anywhere near a population center, then you can expect to have to defend your homestead and your resources from desperate people. In such cases, you should install both passive and physical barriers and early warning devices and systems.

A BUG-IN CHECKLIST

FOOD

I recommend keeping between six months to a year's food supply on hand for each person on average. It needs to be noted that this is only a rule of thumb and it depends completely on where you are and what natural resources are readily available to you. Remember that, on average, men need about 2,500 calories a day and women need around 2,000. Depending on your condition, level of stress, and physical exertion, you may need more.

FOODSTUFFS
- Cooking oils (coconut, vegetable, olive, etc.)
- Cooking powders (flour, baking powder/soda, etc.)
- Dairy products, dry
- Eggs, dry
- Freeze-dried entrees and meals
- Fruit (dried, canned, preserved)
- Grains and cereals
- MREs and other ready-to-eat packaged foods

- Pasta
- Protein, animal (fish, meat, poultry)
- Protein, plant (beans, lentils, nuts, powdered mixes)
- Rice
- Salt, iodized
- Seeds for both consumption and planting
- Soups and stews
- Sweeteners (agave, honey, sugar, etc.)
- Vegetables (dried, canned, preserved)

FOOD PROCUREMENT NEEDS

Hunting and Trapping

- .22 air pellet gun and pellets and gas cartridges
- .22 rifle and ammo
- Compound bow/crossbow and arrows
- Maintenance materials for items in this group
- Rifle and ammo
- Shotgun and ammo
- Traps and snares

The author prepares a squirrel that he harvested, to eat.

The author prepares a rabbit that he harvested to eat.

Knowing how to hunt, trap, and fish can go a long way in keeping you alive when the grocery stores run out of food. In this photo, the author prepares a snapping turtle he caught to eat.

Fishing

- Stocked watering hole or pond
- Natural water source (lake, river, stream, etc.) Compact fishing kit
- Full-size fishing rods and tackle
- Fish Traps
- Fishing Spear Tips

Livestock

Fishing is an outstanding way to supplement your nutritional needs in an emergency.

- Chickens, goats, pigs, cattle, etc .(with the appropriate grazing land and facilities)
- Renewable feed source for livestock
- Renewable water source for livestock
- Full stock of veterinary medications

Farming

- Cultivation equipment
- Adequate fuel storage (with stabilizer)
- Horse-drawn cultivating equipment

Photo Credit: GettyImages

- Manual cultivating tools
- Seed stock
- Hydroponic equipment
- All necessary tools and spare parts needed to maintain and repair farming equipment

WATER

You should have enough potable water to support each person with two gallons per day for hydration, food preparation, and hygiene. Ideally, you would want water stores to come from a renewable

The author drinks from a creek using a Lifestraw water purification straw. While storing water for emergencies is great, you never know when you will have to vacate your location and bug out to a new location. Keeping a portable water filter with your gear makes a ton of sense.

source such as a stream, river, or lake. It is also a good idea to store (with a rotation plan for use) as much water as you can in the event that you need to relocate to an alternate location or if your renewable water source either becomes contaminated or dries up. Store water away from light, chemicals, and pesticides. Don't store any food-grade containers that contain food or water directly on concrete so that contaminants in the concrete do not find their way onto the containers and then possibly into the food or water due to sloppy handling of the containers while opening and closing them. A good technique is to place all of your food and water stores onto a wooden pallet. Always use opaque FDA-approved food grade containers to store your water. I recommend that you cycle your water supply every six months unless you treat it with a water preservative.

WATER PROCUREMENT OPTIONS
- Natural water source (lake, river, well, spring, etc.)
- Solar stills
- Rain catch system
- Hot water tank from house (plus additional water left in plumbing system)

WATER STORAGE OPTIONS

- Individual bottles or cans (store in a cool, dry place such as in closets or under beds)
- Portable water containers (one-, five-, and seven-gallon sizes)
- Static water containers (thirty- and fifty-gallon drums, larger tanks, cistern)
- Water resupply plan (Think this through and devise a plan BEFORE an emergency occurs.)
- Bath tub (Immediately fill your bath tub(s) with water in the aftermath of a disaster or if an emergency situation such as a hurricane landing is imminent.)

Photo Credit: GettyImages

WATER PRESERVATION AND TREATMENT

- Chemical disinfectant supplies
- Heat source and fuel for boiling water
- Ultraviolet water sterilizer

Water filtration systems are great when functioning correctly, but require filter cartridges to be replaced periodically. Be sure to keep spare filters on hand for emergencies. Photo Credit: GettyImages

- Water filters/purifiers
- Water Testing Kits
- Water flavor enhancer to improve the taste of treated water

SHELTER

In an emergency, you are usually better off hunkering down in your home, but a time may come when you need to seek shelter elsewhere. In addition to knowing where local emergency shelters are, you need to have a bug-out plan for a safe location where you can find shelter and security as far away from mass population centers as possible.

HUNKERING DOWN AT HOME

- Fire extinguishers
- Generator, fuel, maintenance tools and materials
- Power inverter
- Smoke and carbon monoxide alarms and batteries
- Wood or manufactured fireplace logs and kindling
- Spare roofing materials
- Spare lumber stores

- Impact/screw drill
- Circular saw with spare blade
- Assorted lubricants, thinners, and other compounds
- Saws, all with multiple blade options
- Spare stores of screws, nails, and hardware
- Full set of carpentry tools
- Metal working and welding equipment
- Chainsaw with spare chain, fuel oil mix, sharpening files, and wrench

FABRICATED SHELTER
- Sleeping bags and ground mats, appropriately sized and insulated
- Tarps, 550 cord, and bungee cords
- Tent replacement and repair parts
- Tent(s) large enough for people, pets, and weather-sensitive gear

LOCAL EMERGENCY SHELTER
- Know the location of the closest emergency shelter

CLOTHING AND EQUIPMENT
- Base layer and street clothing suited to your environment at any time of the year
- Hunting/camouflage clothing and accessories
- Insect- and snake-protective clothing
- Weather-resistant clothing, outerwear, headwear, and footwear

4. SECURITY
Security includes safety issues along with self-defense, making it a very broad category. If you have additional security and safety preparations, you should add them to this list.

HOME SECURITY/EARLY WARNING SYSTEM

- Home alarm
- Motion detectors
- Remote camera systems
- Tangle foot/concertina wire roles
- Trip flares
- Dog(s)

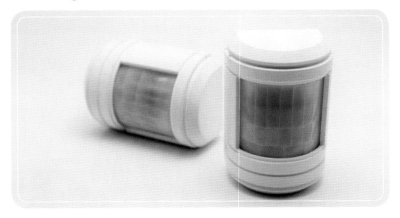

The best offense is a good defense; I recommend having a spectrum of weapons, starting at your non-lethal's such as stunguns and pepper spray and working your way up to handguns for close range and rifles for standoff.

LETHAL WEAPON SYSTEMS

Motion sensor alarms are an inexpensive way to add early warning to your defensive perimeter plan.

- Handgun and spare mags or speed loaders, ammo and accessories
- Rifle and spare mags, ammo and accessories
- Shotgun and ammo

LESS-THAN-LETHAL WEAPON SYSTEMS

- Less-than-lethal shotgun rounds
- Personal defense spray/tear gas dispenser and replacement cartridges
- Restraint systems
- Stun gun and batteries
- Taser and replacement cartridges, batteries, and other accessories

COMMUNICATIONS

- Amateur/HAM radio, CB radio scanner and accessories
- Cell phone and accessories
- Chargers and batteries
- Faraday cage or other protective containers
- FM/AM/SW/weather radio and accessories
- Fire works (mortar tube style, for signaling and early warning)
- Solar-charging panel and accessories
- Television and power source
- Two-way radios and accessories

HEALTH
- Ninety- to 180-day supply of all vital prescription medications
- Sustainable latrine with waste management plan
- Backboard or other litter
- Blankets/space blankets
- Emergency dental kit, per person
- Midwife equipment
- Epinephrine pen kit
- Home first-aid kit
- Individual first-aid kit, per person
- Neck brace and splints

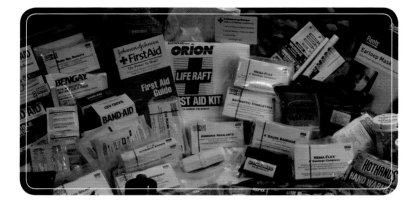

- Personal hygiene kit, per person
- Slings and cravats
- Snake bite kit, per person
- Special medical equipment; defibrillator, CPAP, O2machine and any accessories
- Suture kit
- Trauma kit, per person
- Insect and snake repellant, assorted types
- Mouse traps (and/or cat(s))

POWER
- Gas-powered generator (5k or higher)
- Back-up fuel supply (twenty-five-gallon minimum)
- Fuel stabilizer
- Solar panels with accessories
- Additional alternative power sources such as hydroelectric, wind, or heat.
- Spare batteries and chargers for all of your electronic devices

THE BUG-OUT BAG (BOB): WHAT TO TAKE WITH YOU WHEN YOU HAVE TO GO AND YOU CAN'T COME BACK

Because uprooting yourself and your loved ones and leaving your home, possibly never to return, can be an emotionally charged and complicated endeavor, and will most likely need to be executed

under the most arduous and stressful circumstances imaginable, I have developed this bug-out bag checklist to help simplify and organize your efforts and gear. Whether you're planning to move to safety by vehicle, foot, or other means, this checklist will help you to develop a plan and collect the right gear to protect yourself and your group.

WHAT BACKPACK TO CHOOSE AS YOUR BOB

When it comes to which pack to choose for a bug-out bag, you are sure to hear as many suggestions and opinions as there are different brands and models of bags on the market. Many are geared specifically toward this purpose. I have tried hundreds of bags, and some I liked more than others, but I have always gone back to my ALICE (All-Purpose Lightweight Individual Carrying Equipment load-bearing system) pack when I needed a backpack that I trusted to carry my gear when I could not afford a major malfunction, design flaw, or general comfort issue being a factor. The truth is that the only way to know is to experiment with some different styles and brands of packs and put them through their paces to see which one suits you best.

Note: If you don't want to go through the backpack selection

Photo Credit: GettyImages

process yourself, you can always follow my lead and go with an ALICE pack. These can be purchased online or through a military surplus store and can be found modified with all of the modern materials, extra pockets, and any other add-ons you desire.

WHAT TO PACK IN YOUR BOB

Every BOB is going to be different based on the needs of your group, your individual needs, the distance and type of terrain you will encounter on your journey, and your own physical ability. I suggest that everyone in your group share the burden by ability group, so even small children of walking age would have a bag with some minimal essential and comfort items. I would even suggest that you get your dogs used to carrying food and water on a vest so that they can be prepared to do so in the event of an emergency. The following is a list of generic items to go into a BOB, but I encourage you to modify this list to fit you and your group:

FOOD
- Personal daily rations for three days (or longer, depending on the estimated time of travel to your bug-out location or to a preplanned resupply cache or point)

Photo Credit: GettyImages

- Power bars or meal supplementation bars
- Hard candies
- Broth cubes
- Camp stove (multi-fuel style)
- Camping cook set, utensil, scrubbing pad

WATER
- CamelBak (or similar styled) water hydration system
- Thirty-two-ounce water bottles. (It's recommended that

One way to obtain clean water is to use a pump filtration system. Photo Credit: GettyImages

you drink eight ounces eight times throughout the day, for a total of sixty-four ounces.)
- Water purification tablets or liquid drops
- Water filtration straw or pump-style system
- UV light water purifier

SHELTER

Photo Credit: GettyImages

- Tent, lightweight (terrain and climate dictate style, such as a ground tent, hammock tent, three- or four-season tent, etc.)
- Sleeping bag system (style and rating are climate dependent)
- Poncho liner, military surplus
- Tarp (or US Army poncho) with bungee cords, five to fifty feet of 550 cordage
- Change of clothing (shirt, pants, thermals or under armor, underwear, socks)
- Hiking boots
- Boony hat or ball cap

- Gloves
- Tactical belt

SECURITY

- Carbine or shotgun (with full combat load of ammunition)
- Transition sidearm (semi-auto pistol or revolver with at least one reload of additional ammunition)
- Taser/stun gun combo (for less than lethal option to break contact)
- Pepper spray (for less than lethal option to break contact)
- Flashlight, tactical with extra batteries (500 or more lumens)
- Flex cuffs (several sets)

COMMUNICATION

- Two-way radio (one per member of group)
- Hand-held CB radio
- Hand-held police scanner
- AM/FM short-wave radio and a list of radio stations (plus spare batteries)
- Notepad and pencil

- Calling card
- Stamps and postcards
- Power stick battery charger
- Cell phone and charger cord
- Whistle
- Glow sticks

HEALTH

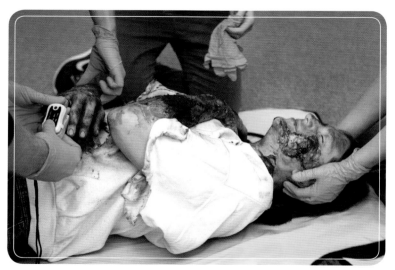

- Chemical protective mask
- Medical face mask
- IFAK/first aid (complete with trauma package/tourniquet/Israeli Bandage as well as other standard first-aid kit items)
- Foot Care Kit (nail clippers, Moleskin, pain relieving ointment)
- Toiletries
- Hand/foot warmers
- Emergency blanket
- Prescription medication (thirty-day supply)

FIRECRAFT

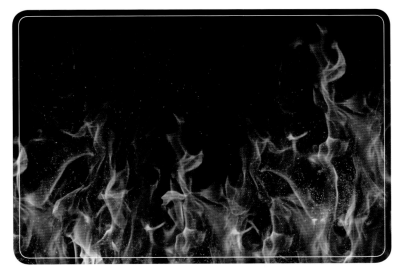

- Ground flares
- Fire-starting kit, complete

LAND NAVIGATION

- Map (road and topographical)
- Protractor
- Map pens
- Compass, lensatic
- GPS

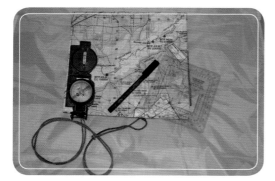

While it is a great idea to have and know how to use a GPS, electronics fail, and usually when you need them the most. Learning navigation skills with a map, compass, and protractor is an absolute must!

MISCELLANEOUS

- Knife (full tang)
- Duct tape
- Black garbage bags
- Leatherman tool
- Religious scriptures (if applicable) and/or other motivational/inspirational reading materials
- Pocketknife/razor blade
- Stress relievers—a favorite book, games, Sudoku, or toys
- An inventory list of everything in your emergency kit

Photo Credit: GettyImages

DOCUMENTS

- Driver's license
- Picture of family members (frontal and profile to assist in search in event someone is lost)
- Credit/debit card and $200 cash (small bills)
- Contact list of family and friends
- Birth certificate
- Marriage certificate

Photo Credit: GettyImages

BUG-IN/BUG-OUT VEHICLE PREPARATION AND MAINTENANCE

In a SHTF scenario, your vehicle may be your life line to getting resupply items, maintaining and moving equipment on your homestead, and getting back to the relative safety of your bug-in location in the event that you run into a problem during an excursion from your property.

If the SHTF, it is imperative that you have a vehicle standing by, packed and ready to go, so that if or when the situation develops to a point where your current location is no longer viable and you need to evacuate to an alternate bug-out location, you won't have to delay your departure preparing your vehicle for movement. Remember, if you make the decision to bug out, you are probably in grave danger and time will be precious.

Readiness Note: Always top off the fuel tank before leaving on an excursion. Don't wait until your gauge hits empty; better to stop and fill up when the tank is half full. Also, keep the vehicle well maintained and always check the tires to ensure that they are operable and properly inflated.

VEHICLE PREPAREDNESS CHECKLIST

In order to ensure that a small problem doesn't snowball into something bigger, I recommend you carry the following items in your vehicle at all times:

- Cell phone (with vehicle charger)
- CB radio
- Police scanner
- Walkie-talkies

Photo Credit: GettyImages

  » AM/FM radio to listen to traffic reports and emergency messages
  » Flashlights and extra batteries
  » Emergency strobe

- » Spotlight (either hand held or vehicle mounted)
- » Emergency signal panel
- » Road flares
- » Reflective triangle
- » Jumper cables
- Fix-a-Flat
- Emergency jump starter
- Small air compressor
- Tow strap (or tow cable)
- Spare tire
- Tire jack with lug wrench
  - » Tire traction straps (or chains)
  - » Spare parts: belts, hoses, fuses, fluids
  - » Folding shovel
  - » Ice scraper
- Local road maps
- First-aid kit (comprehensive)
- One non-perishable meal per person in your party
- One gallon of water per person in your party
- Blanket (wool)
- One or two space blankets
  - » Warm clothes, gloves, hat, sturdy boots, jacket, and an extra change of clothes (in climates where cold weather is an issue)
  - » Baby formula and diapers if you have a small child
  - » Spare gas cans (carry enough fuel to get you to your alternate bug-out location taking into consideration vehicle weight when loaded down and possible detours)

ADDITIONAL ITEMS TO CONSIDER
- Assorted hand tools according to your needs
- Bug-out bag (one per person in your party)
- Bushcraft knife (I suggest carrying more than one knife)
- Survival kit (individual)
- Flashlights and hands-free lights and batteries

- GPS, compass, maps, protractor, marking pens
- Optics for day, night, and thermal, and batteries and accessories
- Pace counter beads
- Wind/waterproof matches, fire starters, tinder
- Windproof lighter and fuel
- Fire arms with combat load of ammunition (one per person in your party if capable.

EMERGENCY PLANS
- Bug-out plan and leave-behind note
- Group emergency preparedness plan
- Local community emergency response team (CERT) point of contact
- Local FEMA/homeland security point of contact
- Local hospital phone number
- Hospital phone numbers along bug-out route
- Phone number and address of local National Guard armory
- Police and fire department phone numbers

WHEN YOU HAVE LITTLE OR NO TIME TO PREPARE

The time to prepare for emergencies is *not* after they happen. If you are reading this book, then hopefully you are a survival-minded

Photo Credit: GettyImages

person and you have already thought out and made arrangements for primary and several alternate locations to bug out to in a SHTF situation. Needless to say, it's always best to have a preplanned bug-out location as well as a preplanned and pre-equipped vehicle to get you there. This is something that happens when it's a perfect world and all the stars align, but since things rarely work out that way, I always suggest to my students that they get into the habit of maintaining an Every Day Carry (EDC) kit so that if the shit hits the fan or they need to break contact quickly, they would at least have a selection of tools and equipment to assist in getting to and surviving in their bug-out destination.

Remember Murphy's Law. Anything bad that can happen will happen at the most inopportune time. That's why having a solid EDC set up and always having a Get-Back-Home Bag (GBH) or a Bug-Out Bag (BOB) fully packed and within a short distance from your immediate location at all times is so vital. And please don't forget to make a comfortable, sturdy pair of walking shoes a part of your BOB (or even EDC) packing list.

Note: The best time to prepare for an emergency is NOT after it happens! Now is the time to plan and coordinate where you will go and how you will get there.

BUG-OUT VEHICLES: HOW TO CHOOSE THE BEST TRANSPORTATION TO GET YOU TO YOUR BUG-OUT LOCATION

The best vehicle to have when the SHTF is the one you have, as long as it works. Remember that the whole philosophy behind preparing to bug out is in pre planning. For your choice of bug-out vehicles, it is particularly important to consider your ability to maintain and repair it and then plan accordingly. I prefer vehicles in the 1990 and earlier class as they tend to be the easiest for even a novice to work on if you are at all mechanically inclined. They have the added benefit of possessing the least number of components that could be fried in the event of an Electromagnetic Pulse (EMP).

I like to apply a P.A.C.E plan (primary, alternate, contingency, and emergency) when it comes to bug-out vehicle selection.

PRIMARY BUG-OUT VEHICLE

Since it is impossible to say exactly what the SHTF event will be, you want your primary bug-out vehicle to cover as many contingencies as possible. For starters, it should be big enough to fit all those you plan to bug out with. Your primary bug-out vehicle should also be able to hold everything you will need as far as food, water, shelter, security, communications, health, fuel, navigational aids, and so on, to get you to your destination, and it should provide adequate protection for any conceivable threats you may encounter. Additionally, it should be powerful and rugged enough to negotiate all of the different types of terrain you could possibly encounter on your way to your bug-out location. You don't need to spend hundreds of thousands of dollars on this; you can easily find an old SUV, truck, or RV in the paper or online and then modify it to fit all of the above specifications without breaking the bank to do so.

ALTERNATE BUG-OUT VEHICLE

Your alternate bug-out vehicle should also be something that can offer protection to your entire party and is capable of getting you from where you are to where you want to go while carrying enough fuel and supplies for each person with you. I have seen set-ups where an RV is able to pull an SUV in tow.

CONTINGENCY BUG-OUT VEHICLE

I suggest that whatever you choose for a contingency vehicle, that you consider finding something that uses an alternative fuel source such as solar power or even pedal power.

EMERGENCY BUG-OUT VEHICLE

The only thing I would say that makes a vehicle fit this category is that you always have it with you. For most of us, this would mean our feet. The reality is that your feet may be all that you have for a bug-out "vehicle" after a catastrophic event occurs, at least initially. Because of this, you should always carry a pair of comfortable and supportive walking shoes at all times. Just ask any of the 9/11 survivors who walked ten to twenty miles from ground zero in business suit attire. Consider it part of your EDC (Every Day Carry). You never know; you may be on the fifthtieth floor of your building in a business meeting when the SHTF and have to walk thirty miles to your home in order to have access to your primary bug-out vehicle.

SHTF FIREARM SELECTION

When it comes to staying alive in a crisis situation or if the SHTF, one of the key factors in your chances of survival could be your availability to a firearm and your ability to use it. From protecting your family from looters and thieves after a major catastrophe to hunting for food to supplement your supply stocks, the right firearm could literally mean the difference between life and death. Consider having the following firearms on hand in your home at all times:

- Pistol: The absolute BEST firearm to have with you in a crisis is the one you have with you, and it is for this reason that the pistol is number one on my list. People will argue

Photo Credit: GettyImages

for the next thousand years over the effectiveness of one caliber to the next but in the end I would just say whatever you decide on, be it a 9mm, a 45 caliber, or whatever, just make sure to have it with you at all times because I promise you the one time you will need it will be the one time you don't have it.

- Shotgun: If not for the fact that it won't fit in your pocket, a shotgun is the ultimate short- to medium-range survival firearm. With a plethora of different ammo types, you can use it for self defense, hunting, breaching, signaling, and all kinds of other applications that can get you out of a jam. I like the 12-gauge mainly because of the ease of availability and versatility of ammo types.

- Medium-Range Assault Rifle: Next on my list would be a medium-range high-capacity rifle such as an AR15- or AK47-style weapon. These weapons are long enough to effectively suppress and engage targets at a relatively high rate of fire and offer you the standoff needed to break contact, as well as being small enough to use when conducting close quarters battle.

- Long-Range Rifle with Scope: I like having a long-range rifle on hand for hunting large game at distance and, in a SHTF scenario, for hitting select targets at ranges out to a thousand meters. You have many choices in this area— 7mm, 7.62, .308, 50 cal—but you want to find a weapon that holds its MOA accuracy and that has a scope powerful enough to be matched with the caliber of ammunition you are using. A round that can fly true at a thousand meters won't matter much if you can't see what you are looking at.
- Low-Caliber Rifle with Scope: I always like to have a small rifle like a .22 caliber on hand because you never know when you may need it to find dinner and the bullets come cheap and come by the thousands. I can put chow in my belly a whole lot faster with a .22 shooting squirrels all year round than I could with the most accurate high-powered rifle trying to hunt big game.

You should stockpile plenty of ammo for whatever weapon systems you choose. You should also take your weapons to the range on a regular basis, both to ensure that they are functioning correctly and to keep yourself proficient. Marksmanship is a perishable skill that needs to be maintained.

Note: While it is your right to own firearms in the US, it is important to remember that with this right comes the responsibility to know how to use them properly and to understand safety precautions as well as the laws in your state. If trying to acquire firearms while residing outside of the US, you may not be able to do so depending on the country you are in. Many countries have much stricter firearm ownership laws than we enjoy here in the United States.

BUG-OUT/BUG-IN LOCATIONS: WHERE SHOULD YOU HOMESTEAD OR BUG OUT TO?

Many people will tell you that if the shit were to hit the fan, they would simply walk off into the wilderness and live off the land.

The fact is that not everyone has the skill sets to actually live off the land and even the very best and most experienced wilderness survival experts are susceptible to Mother Nature's wrath when and if she decides to show her pointy teeth. Even those of us who practice wilderness survival skills on a daily basis would likely not completely cut themselves off

Photo Credit: GettyImages

from society and isolate themselves in the wilderness indefinitely unless the situation was dire. Again, it all comes down to the situation at hand, pre-coordination, preparation, training, and necessity. Planning, equipping, and practicing are the most important aspects of survival, and the extent to which you do so can be directly related to your odds of surviving.

If you are preparing for a SHTF situation, then I suggest you either choose to live in as rural a location as you possibly can, preferably with land that has both the natural resources to help you survive even if you were cut off completely from the power grid, and which provides you with the standoff needed to give you an early warning if and when you are faced with a threat. If homesteading is not a option, then I would suggest either purchasing land in a similar rural setting or finding someone whom you can befriend or offer your skill sets to in exchange for an open invitation to come stay with them in a SHTF situation. If you don't have the money to purchase your own bug-out property and you don't have friends or family you can count on to provide you with a retreat to fall back to, then I suggest you get online and see what is available through the many prepper resources and bug-out websites and chat rooms. I think you will be surprised by how many like-minded people you will find who may be interested in some skill or knowledge you possess and may barter with you in exchange for a spot in their bug-out location.

Photo Credit: GettyImages

Catastrophic Events: How to Survive Man-made and Natural Disasters

Knowing how to stay alive is critical when faced with disaster or catastrophe, be it terrorism, an accident, or a natural occurrence. Preparation by building a disaster kit before disaster strikes and having a good plan that you have rehearsed are the keys to your ultimate survival.

MAKE A FAMILY EMERGENCY COMMUNICATION PLAN (FECP)

The most important thing to consider in the event of any emergency is the safety of your family. We all live active lives and chances are we will not be right next to all of our loved ones at the exact time a catastrophe takes place. Because of this, it is imperative that you prepare and rehearse a Family Emergency Communication Plan so that you are able to ensure that all of your loved ones know what to do and where to go when disaster strikes. Make sure you include a fall-back area in your plan in the event that returning to the house is impractical or impossible. This could be a local school, hospital, police station, or even a storefront or mall. The following factors should be taken into consideration when constructing your plan:

- Who are the members of your family/group who are planning to link up?
- What is each person expected to bring with them?
- What needs to get done prior to linking up?
- Where are you planning to meet?
- What time are you going to meet at that location?
- What will you do if the situation changes or you are not going to make the link-up time?
- What is the load signal (physical signal to let you know who from the group left and where they went)? Try to use a stationary object that can't be easily moved/discarded.
- What is the specific safe and secure bug-out location that you are going to go to? (This will take some pre-coordination. One good technique is to team up with like-minded family and friends who live in remote locations to use as your bug-out destination. If you live in an appropriate place to "bug-in," you can find other family and friends who live some distance from you to use as your bug-out location and they would do the same with you.)

BUILD A DISASTER KIT

Every home should have a basic disaster kit that is tailored to the individual needs of your family. Below I have put together a generic list, but I suggest that you add to it so that it meets your individual needs:

- Water. Two gallons of water per person per day for at least two weeks, for drinking and sanitation.
- Food. At least a two-week supply of non-perishable food.
- Battery-powered or hand-crank radio and a NOAA weather radio with tone alert and extra batteries for both.

- Flashlight and extra batteries
- First-aid kit (see below)
- Whistle to signal for help
- Dust mask. To help filter contaminated air. Also plastic sheeting and duct tape, to shelter in place
- Moist towelettes, garbage bags, and plastic ties for personal sanitation
- Wrench or pliers to turn off utilities
- Can opener for food (if kit contains canned food)
- Local maps
- Prescription medications and glasses
- Infant formula and diapers
- Pet food and extra water for your pet
- Important family documents such as copies of insurance policies, identification, and bank account records in a water-proof, portable container
- Cash, debit/credit card/change
- Emergency reference material such as a first-aid book
- Sleeping bag or warm blanket for each person. Consider additional bedding if you live in a cold-weather climate
- Complete change of clothing including a long-sleeved shirt,

long pants, and sturdy, comfortable walking shoes. Consider additional clothing if you live in a cold-weather climate

- Household chlorine bleach and medicine dropper. When diluted nine parts water to one part bleach, bleach can be used as a disinfectant. In an emergency, you can use it to treat water by using sixteen drops of regular household liquid bleach per gallon of water. Do not use scented, color safe, or bleaches with added cleaners
- Fire extinguisher
- Matches in a waterproof container
- Feminine supplies and personal hygiene items
- Mess kits, paper cups, plates, plastic utensils, paper towels
- Paper and pencil
- Books, games, puzzles, or other activities for children

I suggest that you keep the following items in your first-aid kit at all times:

- Two pairs of Latex or other sterile gloves if you are allergic to Latex
- Sterile dressings to stop bleeding.
- Cleansing agent/soap and antibiotic towelettes
- Antibiotic ointment
- Burn ointment
- Adhesive bandages in a variety of sizes

Photo Credit: GettyImages

- Eye wash solution to flush the eyes or as general decontaminant
- Thermometer
- Trauma kit with tourniquet, Israeli bandage, blood clotting agent
- Epi pen
- Suture kit

MEDICATION

Try to have a thirty- to ninety-day supply of prescription medications that you need to take every day, such as insulin, heart medicine, and asthma inhalers. You should periodically rotate medicines to account for expiration dates. You should also take into consideration prescribed medical supplies such as glucose and blood-pressure monitoring equipment. Additionally, here are some non-prescription drugs and medical supplies to consider including in your disaster kit:

- Aspirin or non-aspirin pain reliever
- Anti-diarrhea medication
- Antacid
- Laxative
- Scissors
- Tweezers
- Tube of petroleum jelly or other lubricant

MAINTAINING YOUR DISASTER KIT

Take the following steps to maintain your disaster kit:

- Keep canned and other extended shelf life foods and water containers in a cool, dry place.
- Store boxed food in tightly closed plastic or metal containers to protect from pests and to extend its shelf life.
- Throw out any canned goods that become swollen, dented, or corroded.
- Establish a rotation system so you can use foods before they go bad and replace them with fresh supplies.
- Keep items in airtight plastic bags and put your entire disaster supplies kit in one or two easy-to-carry containers, such as an unused trash can, camping backpack, or duffel bag. You may not be able to stay at home during a disaster, so having these items stored in a semi-portable fashion will allow you to grab it and go if the emergency situation requires you to quickly leave your home.

Note: You will want to rehearse this routine to make sure the kit fits in your car along with your entire family, pets, etc. Additionally, make sure that your vehicle is always maintained and try to fill up your gas tank every time you get to a half tank. It is also advisable to keep at least ten gallons of gas in your garage. Use the gasoline within six months and switch gas can out for fresh gas to prevent fuel from going bad.

EXPLOSIONS AND EXPLOSIVE DEVICES

Explosive devices are one of the staple tactics used by terrorists today. Be it hidden in a backpack, packed into a vehicle, strapped onto a suicide bomber's body, or in the form of an aircraft being used like a missile, the results are the same and the chances that you have of survival depend almost entirely on where you are in relation to the explosive device when it is detonated. There are a few things that you can do to increase your chances of survival when an explosive is detonated:

- Turn away from the blast when it first goes off. This will protect your eyes and vital organs from flying glass and debris.

Photo Credit: GettyImages

- Drop to the ground with your head facing away from the blast and use your arms to protect your head. As with many of the topics in this book, the best defense against explosives comes with early detection. This is not always easy, as terrorists often plan out their attacks meticulously and accidental explosions often detonate without any warning. You need to have solid situational awareness at all times.
- Bags or boxes left unattended are a key indicator that it may be a bomb. Alert the authorities immediately and move away from the area swiftly.
- Vehicles parked in no parking zones and left unattended are another indicator that should not be ignored. Alert the authorities immediately.
- Suicide bombers often look nervous and can sometimes be recognized as having on an explosive vest under their clothing. Move away from them quickly and alert the authorities immediately.

HOW TO SURVIVE A BUILDING FIRE

One of the most visually disturbing events to come out of 9/11 was when people were literally throwing themselves out of windows and jumping to their deaths to escape the smoke and fire caused by the aircraft striking the towers and exploding. Some situations, like 9/11, are so catastrophic that your ability to escape is strictly based on chance and luck, depending on where you are at the time the catastrophe takes place. All that you can do is plan for every contingency during a fire that is in your control and hope for the best. Above all else, have a plan detailing what to do in the event of a fire. In the special forces, it is often said that the best-laid plans go to hell the second the first round is fired. That may be true, but it is always better to have a plan before emergencies arise than it is to make a plan on the fly. The second effect of an explosion is fire. If you are in a structure such as a building or vessel when an explosion takes place, it is imperative that you understand the actions you need to take to mitigate risk and escape to safety. The American Red Cross

Photo Credit: GettyImages

recommends you take the following precautions if you work or live in a large structure:

- Install smoke alarm and sprinkler systems on every level of the structure. In the US, there are strict fire codes that must be followed.
- Test smoke alarm batteries every month and change them at least once a year.
- Make sure everyone in the building knows at least two ways to escape from every floor of the structure.
- Practice the fire escape plan at least twice a year. Designate a meeting spot outside and a safe distance from the structure. Make sure everyone knows the meeting spot.
- Teach everyone to stop, drop to the ground, and roll if their clothes catch on fire. Practice this on a regular basis.
- Once you get out of the structure, stay out under all circumstances until a fire official gives you permission to go back inside.

- Never open doors that are warm to the touch.
- If smoke, heat, or flames block your exit routes, stay in the room with the door closed. If possible, place a wet towel under the door and call the fire department to alert them to your location in the building. Go to the window and signal for help by waving a bright-colored cloth or a flashlight. Do not break the window, but open it from the top and bottom.
- Never use elevators in the event of a building fire. Use stairs or fire escapes only. Always know where the fire extinguishers are, how to use them, and how to maintain them.

HOW TO SURVIVE A HOME FIRE

Every year over 2,500 people are killed in home fires and thousands more are injured in the United States alone. The following steps should be taken in the event of a home fire:

- Crawl low under any smoke to your exit; heavy smoke and poisonous gases collect first along the ceiling.

Photo Credit: GettyImages

- When the smoke alarm sounds, get out as quickly as you can; you may have only minutes or seconds to safely escape.
- If there is smoke blocking your door or first way out, use your second way out.
- Smoke is toxic. If you must escape through smoke, get low and go under the smoke to your way out.
- Before opening a door, feel the doorknob and door. If either is hot, leave the door closed and use your second way out.
- If there is smoke coming around the door, leave the door closed and use your second way out.
- If you open a door, open it slowly. Be ready to shut it quickly if heavy smoke or fire is present.
- If you can't get to someone needing assistance, leave the home and call 911 or the fire department. Tell the emergency operator where the person is located.
- If pets are trapped inside your home, tell firefighters right away.
- If you can't get out, close the door and cover vents and cracks around doors with cloth or tape to keep smoke out. Call 911 or your fire department. Say where you are and signal for help at the window with a light-colored cloth or a flashlight.
- If your clothes catch fire, "stop, drop, and roll"–stop immediately, drop to the ground, and cover your face with your hands. Roll over and over or back and forth until the fire is out.
- If you or someone else cannot stop, drop, and roll, smother the flames with a blanket or towel.
- Use cool water to treat the burn immediately for three to five minutes. Cover with a clean, dry cloth. Get medical help right away by calling 911 or the fire department.

CHEMICAL, BIOLOGICAL, RADIOLOGICAL, AND NUCLEAR WARFARE-UNDERSTANDING THE CBRN THREAT

Chemical, biological, radiological, and nuclear (CBRN) attacks are a real threat to US infrastructure and to the American population,

Photo Credit: GettyImages

as well as a danger to the rest of the world. Terrorist groups continue to plan CBRN attacks both in the United States and abroad. In order to combat this threat, government agencies have to be successful in their battle to eradicate the CBRN threat, because history proves that terrorists will be unrelenting in their continued attempts to attack.

WHY CBRN ATTACKS ARE SO DANGEROUS

If history is any indicator, it is only a matter of time before terrorists are able to carry out another successful CBRN attack either on US soil or abroad. When a CBRN attack occurs, it is often not easy to understand the nature of the attack. Many chemical agents are colorless and odorless and it is often difficult for medical professionals and authorities to identify that an attack actually took place and then to further investigate the origin of the attack. In some cases, it takes days for symptoms of biological agents to appear in victims, making the origin of the attack even more difficult to identify. A nuclear detonation or even a "dirty bomb" are also real threats that could have catastrophic results if terrorists ever carry out a successful attack.

WHAT TO DO IN THE EVENT OF A CBRN ATTACK

In the event of a CBRN attack, you may take a few simple protective steps. Start observing local wildlife, domestic animals, and livestock. Sick and dead animals are often the first sign that a chemical or biological attack has taken place. If you think it may be a chemical attack, try to stay upwind of the attack. If the attack is radiological or nuclear in nature, find a closed-off shelter and seal up any ventilation ducts, windows, and doors to protect against any fallout. Regardless of what type of CBRN attack has taken place, always cover your mouth and nose to avoid inhaling dangerous toxins or material. Try to cover all exposed skin. Any time skin exposure to CBRN occurs, wash vigorously with warm water and soap. Always know the approved emergency shelters in the area, such as public schools and hospitals. If exposed to CBRN, seek professional help as soon as possible. Listen to public service announcements and try to be patient as the authorities establish decontamination sites, aid stations, and public shelters.

CBRN ATTACK

If you become exposed to a CBRN attack and become ill, standard first aid in many cases will not save you. You must seek out professional medical aid as quickly as possible. Only the military and medical professionals carry the medicines that can help to treat the symptoms of a CBRN attack. This is why it is so important not to get exposed in the first place. If your skin does get exposed, do everything you can to quickly wash it off with mild soap and water. Quickly leave the contaminated area and seek professional medical attention as soon as possible. Do everything in your power not to inhale CBRN agents or to let them get on open skin or in wounds.

MAKING A CBRN SAFE ROOM

Distancing yourself from the CBRN contaminated area is your best chance for survival, but it may not always be possible or practical. If you decide that taking shelter is your only choice, follow this checklist provided by the US Department of State's Bureau of Diplomatic Security:

- Select an inner room on an upstairs floor with the least number of windows and doors.
- Choose a large room with access to a bathroom and preferably with a telephone.
- Avoid choosing rooms with window or wall air conditioners; they are more difficult to seal.
- Close all windows, doors, and shutters.
- Seal all cracks around window and door frames with wide tape.
- Cover windows and exterior doors with plastic sheets (six mil minimum) and seal with pressure-sensitive adhesive tape. (This provides a second barrier should the window break or leak.)
- Seal all openings in windows and doors (including keyholes) and any cracks with cotton wool or wet rags and duct tape. A water-soaked cloth should be used to seal gaps under doors.
- Shut down all window and central air and heating units. Remember to have your disaster kit with you. Be prepared to stay in your safe room for three or more days or until you can be safely evacuated by the authorities. Make sure you have what you need to monitor and communicate with the outside world. A short-wave radio, a TV (if you have power), and a cell phone should all be part of your disaster kit. Keep all the food, water, and other items you will need with you in the safe room, as once you seal off the room you don't want to open it again until the area you are in is clear of contaminants. Don't forget about hygiene products.

CHEMICAL WARFARE

Chemical agents come in four forms:

- Vapors
- Solids

- Liquids
- Gases

Chemical agents include blood, nerve, blister, choking, and metal agents.

NERVE AGENTS:

Signs of mild nerve agent poisoning include, runny nose, drooling, tightness in the chest, cramps, and nausea. Signs of severe exposure to nerve agents are:

- Severe muscular twitching (spasms)
- Loss of bladder and bowel control
- Convulsion
- Unconsciousness
- Respiratory failure (not breathing)
- Strange and confused behavior
- Wheezing, coughing, and gurgling sounds while breathing
- Severely pinpointed pupils
- Red eyes with tears present
- Vomiting.
- If you become exposed to a nerve agent, you must seek out professional medical assistance immediately to receive an Atropine Sulfate injection.

SIGNS AND SYMPTOMS OF METAL AGENTS:

- Cough
- Metallic taste
- Central nervous system effects
- Shortness of breath
- Flu-like symptoms
- Visual disturbances

The primary treatment for most metal agent poisoning is chelation therapy. This needs to be given in pill form or intravenously by a medical professional.

SIGNS AND SYMPTOMS OF BLOOD AGENT INCLUDE:

- Vertigo
- Tachycardia (heart rate faster than normal at rest)
- Tachypnea (rapid breathing)
- Cyanosis (bluish discoloration of the skin and mucous caused by lack of O2 in the blood)
- Flu-like symptoms
- Nonspecific neurological symptoms

At sufficient concentrations, blood agents can quickly saturate the blood and cause death in a matter of seconds to minutes. They cause gasping for air, fierce convulsions, and an excruciatingly painful death. If someone is exposed to a blood agent, get them to professional medical care immediately.

SIGNS AND SYMPTOMS OF CHOKING AGENTS:

- Upper respiratory tract irritation
- Rhinitis (inflammation of the nose or its mucous membrane)
- Coughing
- Choking
- Delayed pulmonary edema (fluid accumulation in the air spaces of the lungs). Treatment for choking agents is rest, warmth, and sometimes steroid therapy. Seek professional medical treatment as soon as possible.

SIGNS AND SYMPTOMS OF BLISTER AGENTS:

Blister agents act primarily on the eyes, respiratory tract, and skin. The eyes are very sensitive and are usually the first to be affected by blister agents.

Signs and symptoms affecting the skin and respiratory tract may not appear for several hours following exposure and include:

- Sensitivity to light
- Itching

- Throat irritation (dry, burning sensation)
- Headache
- Gritty feeling in eyes
- Swelling and redness
- Harsh cough and hoarse voice
- Nausea and vomiting
- Inflammation of the inner eyelids
- Blisters
- Phlegm (mucous discharge) or frothy sputum
- Diarrhea
- Swelling and spasms of the eyelids
- Pain
- Runny nose and frequent sneezing
- Watery eyes
- Pain

HOW TO TREAT A CASUALTY EXPOSED TO A BLISTER AGENT

- Move away from the contaminated area. If you have a protective mask, put it on immediately.
- Quickly flush the victim's eye if liquid blister agent is present in the eye. If agent is present in both eyes, flush both eyes.
- Open an uncontaminated water source like a plastic bottle or canteen.

Photo Credit: GettyImages

- Tilt the victim's head to one side so the eye to be flushed is lower than the other eye.
- Have the victim open his lower eye.
- Pour the water gently into the lower eye, pouring from the inner edge of the eye to the outer edge.
- Continue to flush the eye with water until the blister agent has been flushed from the eye.
- If both eyes are contaminated, tilt the victim's head so the other eye is now lower than the flushed eye and flush the second eye in the same manner.
- Decontaminate the victim's face and exposed skin, then evacuate the casualty as soon as practical.
- If blisters have formed on the victim's unprotected skin anyplace on his body, do not decontaminate or break the blistered areas; you will only spread the contamination. It is particularly important to find medical assistance if the casualty has inhaled blister agents into his respiratory tract, as it can prevent him from being able to breathe.

BIOLOGICAL WARFARE

The three categories of biological agents are:

1. Bacteria
2. Viruses
3. Biological toxins

Bacteria: Anthrax, cholera, plague, tularemia, Q fever
Viruses: Smallpox, Venezuelan equine encephalitis, ebola
Biological toxins: Botulinum toxins, staphylococcal enterotoxin B, ricin, tricothecene mycotoxins (T2).

SIGNS AND SYMPTOMS OF BIOLOGICAL WARFARE AGENTS

Victims displaying symptoms of nausea, difficulty breathing, convulsions, disorientation, or patterns of illness inconsistent with natural disease may have been exposed to a biological agent.

There are a number of medications and antibiotics that can be used to treat biological agent exposure, but they will only work if it is found early enough to do something about it. This is why early detection is so important.

If you think you were exposed to a biological agent, seek professional medical treatment as soon as possible.

Be very cognizant of wildlife and livestock, as they will most likely show signs of the agent first. The best decontamination for a biological agent is warm soapy water.

OTHER SIGNS OF A CHEMICAL OR BIOLOGICAL ATTACK

You need to maintain your situational awareness and understand the indicators that the area that you are in has been contaminated. The key is to put as much distance between yourself and the contaminated area as possible, but you won't be able to do that if you can't read the signs. The US Department of State's Bureau of Diplomatic Security suggests looking out for these additional signs in order to determine if there has been a chemical or biological attack:

- Droplets of oily film on surfaces.
- Unusual number of dead or dying animals in the area.
- Unusual liquid sprays or vapors.
- Unexplained odors (smell of bitter almonds, peach pits, newly mown hay, or green grass).
- Unusual or unauthorized spraying in the area.
- Low-lying clouds or fog unrelated to weather; clouds of dust; or suspended, possibly colored, particles.
- People dressed unusually (long-sleeved shirts or overcoats in the summertime) or wearing breathing protection, particularly in areas where large numbers of people tend to congregate, such as subways or stadiums.

RADIOLOGICAL/NUCLEAR WARFARE

While the initial blast and fire ball that follow a nuclear blast will kill most people exposed to a detonation that are within the kill radius of the blast, the radiological fallout that follows is quite deadly in its own right, depending on how much radiation you absorb. The best thing you can do if you are outside of the blast radius or if there is no blast, such as in the case of a nuclear meltdown, is to seek shelter or to get as far away from the affected area as you can. Symptoms of exposure to radiation include:

- Nausea and vomiting
- Diarrhea
- Headache
- Fever
- Dizziness and disorientation
- Weakness
- Fatigue
- Hair loss
- Bloody vomit and stools
- Infections
- Poor wound healing

Photo Credit: GettyImages

- Low blood pressure
- Death (5.0-6.0 Sv dose or higher). Once you take radiation into your body, it will stay with you for life. There is no cure for a deadly dose (5.0-6.0 Sv) and it is almost always fatal. Lower doses can be treated by medical professionals.

If you think you have been contaminated by radiation, seek medical attention immediately.

HOW TO PLAN FOR A DISASTER

Plan for events that are most likely to affect the area that you are in. If you live in California, for instance, earthquakes are reoccurring events, so you should plan accordingly. Those that live on the coast need to be aware of the possibility of floods and tsunamis. Forest fires plague the Midwestern United States. Terrorism normally occurs in large cities in the US and around the world. If you live near an active volcano, you may want to be prepared to evacuate your home in the event of an eruption. If you live within fifty miles of a nuclear power plant, you may want to know what to do in the event of a meltdown. The key is to try to anticipate events that may occur in the future and then plan on ways to mitigate the risk if that event were to occur. Some common disasters include:

- Earthquake
- Volcano
- Tsunami
- CBRN attack
- Forest fire
- Flood
- Hurricane
- Tornado
- Terrorist attack
- War
- Rioting/looting

- Chaos/anarchy
- Nuclear meltdown
- Chemical spill/fire
- Pandemic

The key is to research the hazards that could most likely affect you so that you know what to do and have a solid and rehearsed plan as well as a disaster kit that fits the hazards you may face.

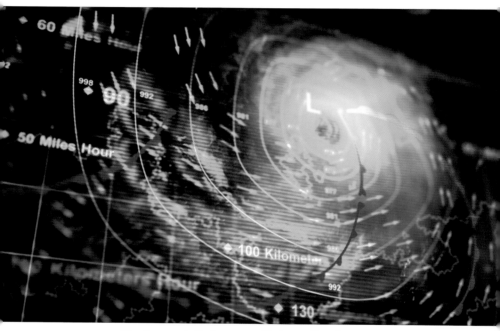

Plan for events that are most likely to affect the area that you are in.

Photo Credit: GettyImages

Extreme Weather Considerations: Cold to Hot and Rain to Snow

EXTREME COLD

Before we talk about cold-weather clothing selection, let's first discuss the different types of cold weather you may encounter.

Photo Credit: GettyImages

Cold weather can be sub-categorized as: wet cold, dry cold, intense cold, and extreme cold.

Often you will encounter several of these conditions, requiring you to be prepared for multiple cold-weather conditions.

Wet, cold conditions occur when temperatures are near freezing and variations in the day and night temperatures cause alternate freezing and thawing. The temperature ranges from 20° to 40°F (-7° to 4°C), not including the wind chill. These conditions are often accompanied by wet snow and rain. During these types of weather scenarios, you should look for clothing that has a waterproof, wind-resistant outer layer, and an inner layer with sufficient insulation to provide protection down to 20°F (-7°C).

Dry cold conditions occur when average temperatures are lower than 20°F (-7°C), the ground is usually frozen, and the snow is dry. Temperatures range from –5° to 20°F (-21° to -7°C) for dry cold, not including wind chill. Insulating layers must protect to –5°F (-21°C). A water- and wind-resistant outer layer must protect these layers.

A good way to check the consistency of snow is to try to make a snowball. If you cannot, then you know the snow is very dry. The wetter snow is, the easier it is to make a snowball.

Intense cold temperature ranges from –5° to –25°F (-21° to -32°C), not including wind chill. Substantial insulating layers are required. All tasks and movement is severely slowed down. Extreme care must be taken to avoid environmental casualties.

Extreme cold temperatures are –26°F (-32°C) and below, not including wind chill. This is the most dangerous sub-category of cold weather and you must be extremely careful when exposing yourself and your gear to these kinds of temperatures. You can expect unprotected gear to fail under these conditions and bodily exposure for any length of time without protection can be fatal.

Now that you know the types of cold-weather conditions you may experience, let's discuss some facts that will allow you to better combat the cold.

To help remember some of the basic principles of how to wear clothing when the temperature is low, you can use the acronym COLD.

C-keep clothing CLEAN; O-avoid OVERHEATING; L-LOOSE and LAYERED; D-keep clothing DRY.

C- Keep Clothing Clean: Clothing keeps you warm by trapping warm air against your body and in the pores of the clothing itself. However, if these pores are filled with dirt, sweat, or other grime, it will not be able to do its job as efficiently.

O- Avoid Overheating: Allowing just enough clothes and body activity to keep you cool, and the environment to cool you down, will keep your clothes from getting sweaty and dirty, and therefore more effective. Overheating can also cause you problems, not with just your clothes. Several cold-weather injuries can be caused by dehydration, hyperthermia, and hypothermia.

L- Loose Clothing/Layering: You want to keep your clothes loose for comfort. If clothing is too tight, it will constrict the flow of blood to your extremities, thereby causing that limb to get cold. Little or no air can be trapped between your body and clothes. It is this warm air that keeps you warm, not the clothes.

Layering: This is another important principle for staying warm in the cold. The more layers, the more warm air can be trapped. Several thin layers of clothing working together will work better than one thick layer working alone.

D- Keep Clothing Dry: You should put on a shell/protective layer gear during sleet or when walking through wet snow. In addition, it helps to take a layer off when you start sweating. Once your clothes are wet, the water or sweat starts to evaporate, drawing off warmth with it.

Layering: A good technique for wearing clothing in cold weather is to utilize a three-layered approach with a vapor transmission layer (moisture wicking), insulating layer, and the protective outer layer (weather+).

Vapor Transmission Layer: Better called a "sweat transfer layer," this is a hydrophobic layer that does not absorb your perspiration. This layer draws moisture away from the skin to keep you dry and warm. Significant progress has been made with synthetics, such as polypropylene, which draws water away from the body, but stays dry.

Insulating Layer: This can be one layer or several layers, which hold the warm air around your body. Preferably, it is lightweight, very compressible, and fast drying. Inner layers are adjusted according to preference, metabolism, and weather conditions to avoid overheating when on the move and cold weather injury when stopped. Take off insulating layers during movement to keep them dry, put the dry insulating layer back on upon stopping. Add or remove insulating layers as needed to avoid sweating and/or chills.

Protective Layer: This protects the insulating layer(s) from getting wet or dirty. In cold-wet environments, it should be made of a wind-proof/water-proof substance.

COLD WEATHER ACCESSORIES

Socks: Socks can help to keep your feet warm and dry while also protecting them from blisters and hotspots if worn correctly. If you're spending a considerable amount of time walking outdoors in

Photo Credit: GettyImages

boots, you should consider wearing a system of two socks on each foot; one thin under-layer sock made from nylon or silk and one thicker insulating acrylic or wool sock. The sock system reduces blisters by allowing friction to occur between the socks instead of the sock and the skin.

The under layer also transports moisture away from the foot to the thicker sock. Keep an extra pair of Merino wool socks in your pack and swap them out when they become sweaty and damp.

Boots: When venturing out into the cold, one of the most critical items of gear that you can have is the proper footwear. You should consider having several sets of boots: one heavier and warmer pair of boots (with a vapor barrier to keep the heat in and the moisture out) for when you are static and not traveling very far on foot or for extreme cold conditions where exposure to the temperature could cause frostbite; and one pair of boots that are designed for long foot movement that provide both warmth and comfort as well as support and flexibility.

If you know you are going to be traveling over snow and ice, you should also consider bringing snowshoes, crampons, ice cleats, and other foot traction devices. In extreme conditions you will want every advantage you can get if you have to travel across icy and snow-covered terrain, particularly if you are in a survival situation.

Leg Gaiters: Gaiters are worn in conjunction with the boots to provide protection from getting snow or debris into the boot itself.

Gloves (cold weather): When you are outside in extreme cold situations, the three most susceptible parts of your body to frostbite are your fingers, toes, and face. To protect your hands, you want a pair of gloves that will provide both insulation and airflow. Consider mitten shells with insulated inserts in extreme cold environments. Gloves should have a wind and waterproof outer layer and an insulated liner or set of inserts.

Hats: You lose the majority of your body heat from your head, and your face is extremely vulnerable to cold weather injury, so it is very important to protect your head and face from extreme cold situations. There are many types of hats out there, but I recommend wearing a multi-purpose hat that can protect your head from heat loss or, if you want to, you can unsnap the ear flaps and protect the sides and back of your head as well. In extreme cold scenarios, consider wearing a neck and face gaiter as well as a pair of snow goggles to completely insulate and protect your entire face.

Sunglasses: You can purchase sunglasses that are specifically designed for use in areas where snow is a prominent part of the outdoor landscape. Snow blindness is a very real problem in high altitude, snow-covered terrain. Even on overcast days, the possibility exists for snow blindness to develop. Always use sunglasses with side shields and that are designed to filter out ultraviolet rays.

Cold Fingers: A good tip for keeping your fingers warm when using gloves is to pull your fingers out of their compartments, keeping them in the gloves, and make a fist. Your warm palm surrounding the fingers will warm them up. It also pays to carry chemically based handwarmers with you at all time.

Note: Put all clothing for the morning inside of your sleeping bag and it will be warm when you wake up.

Food Before Sleep Can Warm You Up: You heat your sleeping bag, not the other way around. Therefore, just before going to sleep, eat something high in carbohydrates to give your body fuel to burn during through the night.

Drink Warm Water to Stay Warm: Fill your canteens and Camelbacks with warm water and keep them in your sleeping bag with you at night. The warm water will help to keep you warm at night and your body heat will keep the canteens from freezing so that you will have water for hygiene, cooking, and drinking when you wake up.

COLD-WEATHER FIRST AID AND HIGH-ALTITUDE SICKNESS

In cold-weather seasons and regions, success and failure are results of the regard that is held for the environment and its dangers.

The person who recognizes, respects, and prepares for these

In extreme conditions where you are maneuvering through extreme cold temperatures and high altitudes, taking rest stops and keeping hydrated is very important. Photo Credit: GettyImages

forces can survive in the most challenging environments and even use these forces to their advantage. The person who disregards or underestimates these forces is doomed to failure, if not destruction.

In extreme cold conditions and wintry, high-altitude environments, care of the body requires special emphasis. If you fail to eat properly or do not get sufficient liquids, efficiency will suffer.

Lowered efficiency increases the possibility of minor to major injuries and can result in death for those who aren't properly prepared.

This will provide you with the information necessary to help prevent, recognize, and treat various health problems that can arise in these challenging and potentially deadly situations. Here are some important considerations to keep in mind when you venture to areas where you may be exposed to cold weather or very high altitudes.

THE FIVE WAYS THE BODY LOSES HEAT

1. Radiation is direct heat loss from the body to its surroundings. If the surroundings are colder than the body, the net

result is heat loss. For instance, a nude man loses about 60 percent of his total body heat by radiation. Specifically, heat is lost in the form of infrared radiation. Bear in mind that in hostile survival situations, infrared targeting devices work by detecting radiant heat loss. Reduce the amount of radiation and reduce your heat signature.

2. Conduction is the direct transfer of heat from an object in contact with a colder object. Most commonly, conduction occurs when an individual sits or rests directly on a cold object such as snow, the ground, or a rock. Without an insulating layer between yourself and the object (such as a sleeping mat), you quickly begin to lose heat.

3. Convection is heat loss to the atmosphere or a liquid, such as water, passing over the surface of your skin. Air and water can both be thought of as "liquids" in this context. Both water and air in contact with the body will absorb heat from the body until it and its surroundings are both the same temperature.

4. Evaporation is when heat is lost when water (sweat) on the surface of the skin is turned into water vapor. This process requires energy in the form of heat, and this heat comes from the body. This is a method the body uses to cool itself, which is why you sweat when you exert yourself. One quart of sweat—which you can easily produce in an hour of hard labor—will take about six hundred calories of heat away from the body when it evaporates.

5. Respiration is a way of losing the body's moisture that most people don't think about. When you inhale, the air you breathe in is warmed by the body and saturated with water vapor. Then, when you exhale, that heat and moisture are lost. That is why your breath can be seen in cold air. Respiration is really a combination of convection (heat being transferred to moving air by the lungs) and evaporation, with both processes occurring inside the body.

THE WINDCHILL EFFECT

Whether walking, skiing, moving in open vehicles, or simply stand-ing in a steady breeze, you must take the wind into account to determine the effective temperature experienced by the unprotected body.

ILLNESS AND INJURY IN EXTREME COLD WEATHER AND HIGH ALTITUDES

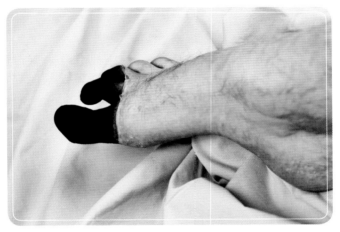

A foot with frostbitten toes. Keeping your feet insulated and dry in extreme cold environments is the only way to prevent frostbite.
Photo Credit: GettyImages

There are several injuries you should be cognizant of when travel-ing in cold conditions. Frostbite and hypothermia are among the most common—and they are dangerous. Additionally, you need to be aware of high-altitude-related sicknesses, which generally occur when people start from sea level or low altitudes and then move quickly to areas at or above 8,000 feet.

Frostbite

Frostbite is the actual freezing of bodily tissue.

Signs and Symptoms: At first, the skin will have a cold and prickly feeling, followed by numbness and red, white, bluish-white, or grayish-yellow skin discoloration, hard or waxy-looking skin, local clumsiness and, in severe cases, blistering after rewarming. Frostbite normally affects the fingers, toes, nose, ears, cheeks, and chin. Frostbite occurs in three stages of severity.

Stage 1: Frostnip is the least severe form of frostbite and can normally be identified by cold, prickly skin that turns pale or red. Frostnip will not do permanent damage to the skin.

Stage 2: Superficial frostbite is a more serious form of frostbite, and you will experience red, white, or pale skin that may remain soft; alternatively, ice crystals might begin to form. At this point, your skin might begin to feel warm. A fluid-filled blister could also appear on the affected area twenty-four hours after rewarming the skin.

Stage 3: Severe (deep) frostbite occurs when the frostbite progresses to its most advanced stages and affects all layers of the skin. After warming, large blisters will form, followed by the skin turning black in the affected areas. As necrosis continues, the affected tissue will die and fall off.

Prevention: Limit your time in the cold, follow the COLD acronym when you dress, and don't expose your skin to extreme cold or to windchill.

Treatment: Frostbite is treated by slowly re-warming the skin, removing any dead tissue, and preventing infection. This is best done by qualified medical personnel.

Hypothermia

Hypothermia occurs when the body loses heat faster than it can produce it, and core temperature falls to 95°F or below. The causes of hypothermia are low ambient temperature, windchill, wet clothing, cold-water immersion, improper clothing selection, exhaustion, alcohol intoxication, and use of nicotine and certain drugs.

Signs and Symptoms: There are a number of signs and symptoms of hypothermia. Some of the most indicative are intense and/or violent shivering, muscular rigidity with puffy, blue skin, slurred speech or mumbling, slow, shallow breathing or respiratory and cardiac failure, weak pulse, clumsiness or lack of coordination, drowsiness or very low energy, confusion or memory loss, loss of consciousness and cold, bright-red skin (in infants).

Prevention: Some ways to prevent hypothermia include wearing proper cold-weather clothing fit for the environment, keeping yourself and your clothing dry, avoiding dehydration, eating adequately, avoiding fatigue and exhaustion, increasing your activity as the temperature drops, and never eating snow as a means to stay hydrated.

Treatment: It is difficult to diagnose yourself for hypothermia, but once it is discovered, the first thing to do is prevent further heat loss. Get the victim out of the cold as soon as possible. Insulate the victim and warm them by unclothing them—and yourself—and huddling together inside a sleeping bag or under several blankets. If possible, call 911 immediately and evacuate the victim to a medical facility for further treatment.

High-Altitude Illness

High altitude, in this regard, is considered to be from 4,921 to 11,483 feet above sea level. Individual tolerance to altitude varies, and one can suffer different effects at the same elevation at different times, making activity at higher altitudes difficult to plan for.

Signs and Symptoms: The signs and symptoms of high-altitude sickness are varied, but some common indications are a persistent headache, shortness of breath unrelated to exertion, dry cough, extreme lack of energy, nausea, inability to sleep, lack of appetite and/or a loss of balance. In some cases, symptoms might abate after several days at altitude.

Prevention and Treatment: Time should be taken to acclimate to traveling at high elevations, and one should expect to reduce activity during this time.

Generally, when one is above 8,000 feet, the best chance for survival is to descend to a lower elevation. Failure to do so could lead to more serious illnesses such as Acute Mountain Sickness (AMS), High Altitude Pulmonary Edema (HAPE), and/or High Altitude Cerebral Edema (HACE).

While there are many dangers associated with being in extreme cold-weather environments and traveling to high elevations, proper preparation can mean the difference between success and disaster.

WARM WEATHER CONSIDERATION AND INJURY PREVENTION

Photo Credit: GettyImages

EXTREME HEAT

Let's discuss the different types of warm weather you may encounter. Warm weather can be sub-categorized into dry heat and humid heat. Temperatures in arid and dry locations can climb as high as

55° C (130° F) during the day and rapidly drop down to as low as 10° C (50° F) at night. This extreme shift in temperature can chill you to the bone if you don't have the correct clothing.

DRY HEAT:

Dry heat normally occurs in arid environments. Dry heat can be particularly dangerous because it is often accompanied with unblocked wind that dries the sweat immediately, making it difficult to realize how much water you are actually losing, which can lead to dehydration. Arid environments are usually barren of water and vegetation with only sparse resources for a survivor to depend on. Arid land can range from sand dunes deserts to flat dry lake beds or tall treeless mountains with temperatures that are as extreme as the land itself. Bringing the proper food, water, clothing, and shelter with you is most important when traveling in arid environments.

HUMID HEAT:

In humid, mainly forested environments and/or high vegetation, sub-tropical and tropical environments with altitudes ranging from sea level swamps to high mountain triple canopy jungle. In these humid regions, summer temperatures can range from between 50° F and 105° F. Summertime weather also often includes high humidity and heavy rainfall, so you should consider the specific weather patterns in the area you are traveling to before you decide on what clothing to bring on your excursion.

HOT WEATHER CLOTHING AND PROTECTIVE GEAR SELECTION

When traveling to high heat climates, you should consider wearing clothing that is lightweight, loose fitting, and with colors that are on the lighter side of the spectrum, since darker colors are known to absorb the sun's heat.

Shirts: Contrary to popular belief, wearing a T-shirt or not wearing a shirt at all in high heat situations when the sun is blaring down on you is not always the best way to cool your body and protect yourself from the harmful rays of the sun. In areas of high heat and low humidity, look for shirts with long sleeves and light colors. If you are a woman and you need an undergarment to wear under your shirt, look for a bra that will not cause you to rash in the high heat and that provides your body with good ventilation. As for fabrics to use in hot weather environments, there are several. Cotton is one of those fabrics that most people would suggest wearing in the heat because it soaks up all of the perspiration from your body and allows it to evaporate slowly.

It further allows the heat to be wicked away from your skin. One of the problems with cotton is that it tends to bunch up and cause chafing when it gets wet. While cotton is not a bad choice, there are other options.

There have been some amazing advances in fabric technology, due mainly to research and development resulting from almost two decades of continuous wars being fought by our military in very extreme high and low temperature environments. Some of the polyester-based knits being used to make clothing these days will do an excellent job at letting moisture from your sweat evaporate quite quickly, which in turn will help to keep you much cooler when you are moving and will then dry quickly when you stop. There are even some wool fabrics out there that will help keep you cool from the summer heat. Merino wool, for instance, has small "pockets" woven into the fabric that absorb water and then allow it to seep out slowly, which will help greatly in keeping your body temperature down. An added bonus of wool is that it does not do well at absorbing body odor (if that is one of your concerns).

Pants: For pants, you should follow the same rules as you did for shirts by selecting fabrics that are lightweight, loose fitting, and have light colors. Look for pants that perform multi-functions, such as pants with removable pant-legs that transform them into shorts. Pants that have multiple pockets with Velcro or zipper flaps are an added bonus, as you will have places to secure your gear and valuables.

Shoes: Boots are without a doubt one of the most important pieces of clothing and equipment that you can have when you are spending time in the outdoors and you are putting a considerable amount of mileage on your feet. A good pair of boots can make the difference between an enjoyable experience and a nightmare scenario where every step brings excruciating pain. A survival situation only compounds the need for a pair of shoes that fit correctly and are designed to handle any abuse that you put on them, without failure. When searching for the right pair of outdoor hiking boots, fit is everything. To find the right fit, you first want to ensure that the "last," which is the wooden foot that the manufacturer chooses to build the shoe around, is a match for your individual foot size.

If you try on a shoe and your foot either has way too much room to move around or your foot seems to swell over the shape of the bottom of the shoe, then the last is most likely not a good fit for you. What you want is a shoe that is snug around your foot with a hiking sock on. If you are buying boots and your feet are not swollen from walking, wear a thicker pair of socks to represent your foot size after you have been walking on them for some time. If you can't find a pair of shoes that seem to fit the way you want them to, consider seeing your podiatrist to get custom-made orthotics. Blisters, which are caused by friction between your foot and your boot or sock, are one of the biggest problems that the wrong shoes and socks can cause.

Hats: While many people think that hats worn in the summertime only provide the eyes with relief from the sun's rays and assist in keeping sweat from running down your face, the fact is that cooling technology has actually come a long way. In fact, several hat and garment makers now use fabrics that provide evaporative cooling technology and assist in keeping the body temperature down.

Raingear: Raingear is always a good thing to have with you whether you are venturing out into the wilderness or simply driving to work. while raingear comes in many forms and configurations, from two-piece to jump suits to ponchos, all raingear has one thing in common: they all provide a non-porous waterproof surface that will protect you from the rain, snow, ice, and wind. We are often confused when searching for raingear between the terms "waterproof" and "water resistant." While water resistant will help to keep you dry, it is not waterproof and it will eventually succumb to heavy rain, leaving you soaked through. The reason people choose water resistant over waterproof is that waterproof materials will not allow your body to wick off perspiration when you are moving, increasing the possibility that you could experience discomfort or even cold injury if you don't find another way to dry off or keep warm.

That said, if you are in a stationary or "static" position where activity is limited, it is smart to have a set of waterproof raingear to put on in order to keep you dry when the rain comes down. Waterproof ponchos have the added benefit of making great shelter tops when getting yourself out of the elements.

Work Gloves: The idea behind finding the perfect pair of gloves seems simple but in fact it is not that easy. In reality, you may need to have several different pairs of gloves depending on what you are doing. An easy way to classify what gloves you need for the job is to assess the importance of the following areas and then determine which gloves are the best for you:

- Durability and protection
- Fit and dexterity
- Comfort and aesthetics

You may find it difficult to find one single set of gloves that meets all of the above-mentioned criteria equally. For instance, while a form-fitting pair of leather gloves will provide excellent protection from friction and heavy labor-intensive work, they will not do a great job at keeping your fingers warm in winter. Again, you may need to get either several pairs of gloves or look for a glove system that can be modified to meet several criteria by simply switching out with different system components for different activities.

Hiking Boots and Camp Shoes: Much like gloves, hiking boots are not an easy thing to choose, as it is rare to find a single pair of shoes that will do a good job at every activity you may find yourself doing. What you want to do is to look for a high-cut, full-grain leather hiking boot to offer you maximum ankle support and durability when traveling on foot in the wilderness. For short walks around your campsite, you can get a second pair of boots with a low or mid-cut for adequate but not superior ankle support and made from a more breathable synthetic or leather-synthetic mix. You may also want to consider a third pair of shoes designed specifically for protecting your feet in the water if you expect to be walking across water obstacles, fording rivers, or searching for food in streams and creeks. A good shoe for this is either a well-made pair of waterproof sandals or a good pair of water shoes.

Socks: The same factors apply to socks regardless of the temperature. You naturally don't have to worry so much about the insulating qualities of your socks in the summertime, and you want a sock that will allow your feet to sweat and that wicks away any remaining moisture so that your feet remain dry.

Sunglasses: While the range of sunglass quality and price is quite large, the only factor that really matters when looking for a good pair of sunglasses is if they block 100 percent of UV rays from the sun. When you see the word "Polarization" on your sunglasses, it simply means that the glasses are designed in such a way that they can reduce the amount of glare that comes off reflective surfaces such as water or pavement.

Photo Credit: GettyImages

HOT-WEATHER INJURY PREVENTION AND TREATMENT
The three most common heat-related injuries are:

- Heat cramps
- Heat exhaustion
- Heat stroke

To stay properly hydrated, you should drink at least two liters of water per day (or approximately half a gallon), but that's an average figure and it depends upon your age, gender, physical condition, and circumstances.

For example, you'll require way more than two liters of water per day if you're hiking in scorching heat or if you're working out, rather than staying indoors in a house without air conditioning, etc. That's common sense, though.

Photo Credit: GettyImages

If you don't drink enough water to replace the loss of fluids that occurs via sweating, you'll put your body in a state of emergency, as your body is losing salt and water and not getting enough electrolytes.

Salt, magnesium, and potassium imbalances caused by dehydration may cause cramps, cardiac arrhythmia, dizziness, and confusion–basically your brain doesn't work right.

For people who aren't used to heat, there's also always the risk of heat edema and, worst-case scenario, a fatal heat stroke when your body gives up and stops sweating. This occurs when you're exposed to extreme heat for long periods of time and is called anhidrosis.

However, the most common problems that occur during a summer heat wave are heat cramps and heat exhaustion.

As the body starts to dehydrate and lose salts, it is not uncommon to experience abdominal cramps as well as cramps affecting the extremities. These are commonly referred to as "heat cramps."

Heat exhaustion is a consequence of one's body losing significant amounts of salt and water; sans electrolytes, the body can't cope with heat anymore. Salt and potassium are the two primary minerals that control your blood pressure, and when you sweat, they're two of the first that you lose.

Obviously, heat exhaustion and all heat-related ailments are particularly dangerous in a survival situation, such as when you're outdoors hiking, climbing, or whatever.

Heat exhaustion's first symptom is when your core temperature rises above 98.6° F, your normal body temperature. This results in intense thirst, heavy sweating, dizziness, and an overwhelming feeling of fatigue. Your body is literally starting to cook.

The first thing that you need to do is get out of the heat if possible and hydrate. Avoid strenuous activities during the day in open sunny spots, especially if there's a heatwave warning.

If heat exhaustion sets in, you must find a cool, shaded location and remove the victim's clothes, including (especially) the shoes and socks then, apply wet clothes to the victim's face, head, neck, and, if possible, their feet.

Spray with cool water if possible. Encourage the victim to drink as much water as possible. Sport drinks (if available) are great, as they contain minerals and vitamins (the famous electrolytes included) together with sugar, which gives the body a boost.

Try to get medical aid as soon as possible, especially if you spot the early signs of a heat stroke (way worse than heat exhaustion), which include:

- Profuse sweating
- Hot, dry skin
- A core temperature of around 104° F (or higher)
- Feeling cold (yes, it seems strange, but it's a fact)
- Loss of consciousness, and/or seizures

All of these symptoms are signaling that the body's mechanisms for coping with heat have failed and the victim is at the death's door. Heat strokes are very serious, with a mortality rate of about 10 percent, and yes, people really do die in extreme heat conditions. It's not rare.

Most people who die during heat waves are elderly folk living in big cities in the upper floors of buildings, especially old, inadequately ventilated apartment buildings. In the US alone, over 600 people die annually, and thousands visit emergency rooms due to extreme heat conditions.

Since we've already established that heat is a silent killer, as the weather gets more extreme, avoid the main danger by staying out of the sun. If you're outdoors on foot, avoid traveling during the day, and do it by night, like Bedouins. If you find yourself traveling or lost in the wilds in the heat, drinking lots of water and covering your head and your entire body in white (best case scenario) sheets would go a long way toward preserving your body's reserve of electrolytes if traveling during the day.

The rule of the thumb is that when your core temperature gets above 104° F, you're in serious trouble. Obese and elderly people are especially vulnerable to heat, and small children have tiny hearts, which are not always capable of cooling their bodies efficiently. Kids also have a slow sweat response, which puts them in danger in extreme situations.

MORE HINTS ON SURVIVING THE HEAT

- Try to avoid caffeine and alcoholic beverages (they act as diuretics) during heat waves
- Maintain a proper level of hydration at all times
- When indoors, try to eliminate extra sources of heat (computers and appliances left running, etc.)
- Don't eat big, protein-rich meals, as they warm the body by increasing metabolic heat. Be ready to recognize the early symptoms of heat exhaustion and heat stroke and take action.

Photo Credit: GettyImages

Appendix A

WORLDWIDE EMERGENCY CONTACT INFORMATION FOR US CITIZENS

For more detailed information about individual embassies and consulates worldwide including:

- Current travel warnings
- Country specific information
- Travel alerts
- Emergency contact information

Go to: http://www.usembassy.gov

EMBASSY AND CONSULATE CONTACT INFORMATION

US Embassy/Consulate Emergency Contact Telephone Number List (please note that these numbers are subject to change).

Afghanistan Kabul-[93] (2) 290002, 290005, 290154

Albania Tirana -[355] (4) 247-285 thru 89

Algeria Algiers -[213] (21) 69-12-55, 69-32-22, 69-11-86, 69-14-25

Angola Luanda -[244] (2) 447-028/445-481

Argentina Buenos Aires -[54] (11) 5777-4533 Armenia Yerevan -3741-151-551

Australia Canberra -[61] (2) 6214-5600, after hours Tel 6214-5900; Melbourne -[61] (03) 9526-5900, after hours Tel 9389-3601; Perth -[61] (8) 9202-1224, after hours Tel 9476-0081; Sydney -[61] (2) 93739200, after hours Tel 4422-2201

Austria Vienna -[43] (1) 31339. Consulate: 31339-75-35, After hours call Duty Officer 31339; Salzburg -[43] (0662) 8487-76, After-Hours Emergencies—Call Vienna Duty Officer 31339

Azerbaijan Baku -[9] (9412) 98-03-35, 36, 37

Bahamas Nassau -(242) 322-1181, after hours Tel 328-2206

Bahrain Manama -[973] 273-300, after hours Tel 275-126
Bangladesh Dhaka -[880] (2) 882-4700-22

Barbados Bridgetown -(246) 436-4950, Fax 429-5246 and
429-3379

Belarus Minsk -[375] (17) 210-12-83 and 234-77-61, after hours
Tel 226-1601

Belgium Brussels -32] (2) 508-2111

Belize Belize City -[501] (2) 77161 thru 63

Benin Cotonou -[229] 30-06-50, 30-05-13, 30-17-92

Bermuda Hamilton -[441] 295-1342

Bolivia La Paz -[591] (2) 430251;

Cochabamba -[591] (4) 116313; Santa Cruz -[591] (03)363842,
330725

Bosnia and Herzegovina Sarajevo -[387] (33) 445-700

Botswana Gaborone -[267] 353-982, after hours Tel 357-111 or
374498

Brazil Brasilia -[55] (61) 312-7000; Belem -[55] (91) 242-7815;
Fortaleza -[55] (85) 252-1539; Manaus -[55] (92) 633-4907;
Porto Alegre -55] (51) 3225-2225/3226-3344; Recife -[55] (81)
3421-2441, Emergency Tel 3421-5641; Rio de Janeiro -[55]
(21) 2292-7117; Salvador da Bahia -[55] (71) 345-1545; Sao
Paulo -[55] (11)3081-6511

Brunei Bandar Seri Begawan -[673] (2) 220-384, 229-670, After
hours emergency [673] (8) 730-691

Bulgaria Sofia -[359] (2) 937-5100

Burkina Faso Ouagadougou -(226) 30-67-23, after hours Tel
31-26-60 and 31-27-07 Burundi Bujumbura -[257] 22-34-
54, after hours Tel 21-48-53 Cambodia Phnom Penh -[855]
23-216-436/438

Cameroon Yaounde -(237) 223-40-14, or (237) 222-25-89

Canada Ottawa, Ontario -(613) 238-5335; Calgary, Alberta -(403)
266-8962; Halifax, Nova Scotia -(902) 429-2480;

Montreal, Quebec -(514) 398-9695; Quebec, Quebec -(418) 692-2095;

Toronto, Ontario -(416) 595-1700; Vancouver, British Columbia -(604) 685-4311; Winnipeg, Manitoba-(204) 940-1800

Cayman Islands Georgetown, Grand Cayman-(345) 945-1511

Central African Republic Bangui -[236] 61-02-00, 61-02-10, 65-25-78, After hours phone (236) 50-12-08 Chad N'Djamena -[235] (51) 70-09, 51-90-52, 51-92-33 Chile Santiago -[56] (2) 232-2600

China Beijing -[86] (10) 6532-3831; Chengdu -[86] (28) 558-3992, 558-9642, Duty Officer Tel 1370-800-1422; Guangzhou -[86] (20) 8188-8911, Duty Officer Tel.139-0229-3169; Shanghai -[86] (21) 6433-3936; Shenyang -[86] (24) 2322-0848 or 1198, Duty Officer Tel 137-0988-9307

Colombia Bogota -[57] (1) 315-0811, Consulate Tel. 315-1566; Barranquilla -(95) 353-0970 or 0974

Congo Brazzaville Brazzaville -(co-located with Kinshasa embassy) [243] (12) 21532, 21807, cellular line: [243] (88) 43608; Consulate (88) 46859

Congo Kinshasa Kinshasa -[243] (12) 21532, 21807, cellular line: [243] (88) 43608; Consulate (88)46859 Costa Rica San Jose -(506) 220-3939, after hours Tel 220-3127

Cote d'Ivoire Abidjan -[225] 20-21-09-79 or 20-21-46-72

Croatia Zagreb -[385] (1) 661-2200, after hours Tel 661-2400

Cuba Havana-(Swiss Embassy) 53] (7) 33-3551/9, 33-3543/5, after hours Marine Post 1 33-3026

Cyprus Nicosia -[357] (22) 776400, after hours Tel 776934

Czech Republic Prague -[420] (2) 5753-0663

Denmark Copenhagen -[45] 3555-3144, after hours Tel 3555-9270

Djibouti Djibouti -[253] 35-39-95, after hours 35-13-43

Dominican Republic Santo Domingo -[809] 221-2171, after hours Tel 221-8100 or 562-3560; Puerto Plata-[809] 586-4204 Ecuador Quito -[593] (2) 2562-890, after hours Tel 256 1-749; Guayaquil -[593] (4) 2323-570, After-hours Tel 2321-152

Egypt Cairo -[20] (2) 797-3300 El Salvador San Salvador -(503) 278-4444

Eritrea Asmara -[291] (1) 120004

Estonia Tallinn -[372] 668-8100, Duty Officer Cell Phone Tel [372] (5) 092-129

Ethiopia Addis Ababa -251] (1) 550-666

Fiji Suva -[679] 314-466

Finland Helsinki -[358] (9) 171-931

France Paris -[33] (1) 4312-2222; Bordeaux-[33] (5) 5648-6380; Lyon -[33] (4) 7838-3688 or 7838-3303; Marseille -[33] (4) 9154-9200; Martinique -596-71-9690; Strasbourg -[33](3) 88-35-31-04; Toulouse-[33] (5) 3441-3619

Gabon Libreville -[241] 74-34-92, 76-20-03/04, 72-12-39/41

Gambia Banjul -(220) 392-856, 392-858, 391-970, 391-971

Georgia Tbilisi -[995](32) 989-967; Emerg 922-832 Germany Berlin -[49] (30) 238-5174; Dusseldorf -[49] (211) 788-8927, after hours [49] (0172)970-2456; Frankfurt Am Main -[49] (69) 75350; Hamburg -[49] (40) 41171-100, after hours Tel [49] (173) 208-3038; Leipzig -[49] (341) 213-840; Munich -[49] (89) 2888-0, after hours Tel [49] (171) 815-4805

Ghana Accra -[233] (21) 775-347/8/9

Greece Athens -[30] (10) 721-2951; Thessaloniki -[30] (31) 242905 or 720-2400 Grenada St. George's -[473] 444-1173/6

Guatemala Guatemala City -(502) 331-1541

Guinea Conakry -[224] 41-15-20, 41-15-21, or 41-15-23

Guyana Georgetown -[592] (2) 54900-9, and 57961-3

Haiti Port-au-Prince -[509]222-0354, 222-0368, 222-0200, 222-0612

Honduras Tegucigalpa -[504] 238-5114 or 236-9320, after hours Tel. 236-9325

Hong Kong Hong Kong -[852] 2523-9011(after hours/emergency: 2841-2230)

Hungary Budapest -[36] (1) 475-4400

Iceland Reykjavik -[354] 562-9100 India New Delhi -[91] (11) 2419-8000, 2 611-3033; Calcutta -[91] (33) 2282-3611 thru 15, and 2282-5757; Chennai -[91] (44) 2811-2000, 2811-2008, 2811-2009; Mumbai -[91](22) 2363-3611 through 23633618

Indonesia Jakarta -[62] (21) 3435-9000; Bali -[62] (361) 233-605; Surabaya -[62] (31) 567-6880 or 568-2287

Ireland Dublin -[353] (1) 668-8777, after hours Tel 668-9612

Israel Tel Aviv -[972] (3) 519-7575, after hours Tel 519-7631; Haifa -[972] (04) 670615; Jerusalem -[972] (2) 622-7230, after hours Tel 6227250

Italy Rome -[39] (06) 46741; Florence -[39] (055) 239 8276/7/8/9, 217-605; Milan -[39](02) 290-351, Consulate 290-35300; Naples -[39] (081) 583-8111, or 583-8245; Palermo -[39] (091) 305-857, after hours/ emergencies Tel (081) 583-8111; Trieste -[39] (040) 660-177, Home 302-354

Jamaica Kingston -(876) 929-4850 thru 9; Montego Bay -(876) 9520160/5050

Japan Tokyo -[81] (3) 3224-5000; Fukuoka -[81] (92) 751-9331/4; Nagoya -[81] (52) 203-4011; Naha, Okinawa -[81] (98) 876-4211; OsakaKobe -[81] (6) 6315-5900; Sapporo -[81] (11) 641-1115/7;

Jordan Amman -[962](6)592-0101, After hours number to Post 1 [962](6)592

Kazakhstan Almaty -[7] (3272) 633921, 631375, or 507623, after hours Tel 507627

Kenya Nairobi -[254] (2) 537-800, after-hours number 537-809

Kosovo Pristina-[381](38)549-516, Satellite Tel 873-761-912-435, after hours 377-044-153-594 Kuwait Kuwait -[965] 539-5307/5308, after hours 538-2097/2098

Kyrgyz Republic Bishkek -[996] (312) 551-241, (517) 777-217, night/ emergency numbers (312) 551-262

Laos Vientiane -[856] (21) 212581/582/585, after hours Tel 212581

Latvia Riga -[371]703-6200

Lebanon Beirut -[961] (4) 543-600, 542-600, 544-130/131/133

Lesotho Maseru -[266] 312-666

Liberia Monrovia -[231] 226-370-380

Lithuania Vilnius -[370] (2) 665500

Luxembourg Luxembourg -[352] 460123 Macedonia Skopje -[389] 116-180

Madagascar Antananarivo -[261] (20) 22-21257 or 22-20956,

Cellular [261] 030-23-80900 Malawi Lilongwe -[265] 773-166, 773-342, 773-367

Malaysia Kuala Lumpur -[60] (3) 2168-5000

Mali Bamako -223] 225470, after hours Tel 223833 Malta Valletta -[356] 21- 235-960

Marshall Islands Majuro -(692) 247-4011

Mauritania Nouakchott -(222) 525-2660/63, 525-1141/45, 525-3038 after hours Tel 525-3288

Mauritius Port Louis -[230] 202-4400; 208-2347

Mexico Mexico City -52] (5) 080-2000; Acapulco -[52] (74) 81-16-99; Cabo San Lucas - (114)33566; Cancun -[52] (98) 83-2450; Ciudad Juarez -[52] (16) 11-3000; Cozumel-[52] (987) 245-74; Guadalajara -[52] (33) 3825-2998, 3825-2700; Hermosillo -[52](62) 17-2375; Ixtapa -(52) (755) 3-1108, Cell 7-1106; Matamoros -[52] (868)-8124402; Mazatlan -[52] (69) 165889/134444, ext. 285; Merida -[52] (99) 255011; Monterrey -52] (8) 345-2120; Nogales, Sonora -[52] (63) 134820; Nuevo Laredo -[52] (87) 14-0512; Oaxaca -[951] 43054; Puerto Vallarta -[52] (322) 2-00-69; San Luis Potosi -[52] (48) 117802; San Miguel de Allende -(415) 22357; Tijuana -[52](6) 681-7400

Micronesia Kolonia -[691] 320-2187

Moldova Chisinau -[373] (2) 233-772, after hours Tel 237-345 Mongolia Ulaanbaatar -[976] (11) 329095

Morocco Rabat -[212] (3) 776-2265, after hours Tel 776-9639; Casablanca -[212] (2) 226-4550 Mozambique Maputo -[258] (1) 492797

Myanmar Rangoon -[95] (1) 282055, 282182

Namibia Windhoek -[264] (61) 221-601

Nepal Kathmandu -[977] (1) 411179

Netherlands The Hague -[31] (70) 310-9209; Amsterdam -[31] (20) 5755-309

Netherlands Antilles Curacao -[599] (9) 461-3066 New Zealand Wellington -[64] (4) 462-6000; Auckland -[64] (9) 3032724 Nicaragua Managua -[505] (2) 66-2298, 666010, 666012/13, 66601518, 666026/27, 666032/33

Niger Niamey -[227] 722661 thru 4, after hours Tel 723141

Nigeria Abuja-[234] (09) 523-0916/0960/5857/2235;

Lagos -[234] (1) 261-0050

Norway Oslo -[47] 2244-550

Oman Muscat -[968] 698-989, after hours Tel [968] 699-049

Pakistan Islamabad -[92] (51) 2080-0000; Karachi -[92] (21) 568-5170 thru 79; Lahore -[92](42) 636-5530 thru 5540; Peshawar -[92] (91) 279801/03, 285496/97 Palau Koror -(680) 488-2920/90 Panama Panama City -[507] 207-7000

Papua New Guinea Port Moresby -[675] 321-1455

Paraguay Asuncion -[595] (21) 213-715

Peru Lima -[51] (1) 434-3000, after hours Tel 434-3032; Cuzco -[51] (84) 24-5102

Philippines Manila -[63] (2) 523-1001; Cebu -[63] (32) 311-261/2; 2310-671

Poland Warsaw -[48] (22) 628-3041, after hours Tel 625-0055, 6250133, 629-0638, or 629-3651; Krakow -[48] (12) 424-5100; Poznan -[48] (61) 851-8516

Portugal Lisbon -[351] (21) 727-3300; Funchal -[351] (91) 743-429; Ponta Delgada -[351] 296-282216

Qatar Doha -[974]488-4101

Romania Bucharest -[40] (1) 210-4042, emergency after hours 2100149

Russia Moscow -[7] (095) 728-5000, emergency after hours Tel 7285025; St. Petersburg -[7] (812) 275-1701, after hours Tel 274-8692; Vladivostok -[7] (4232) 300070 (Note: if calling from the US, or the U.K., dial [7-501] (4232) 300072); Yekaterinburg -[7] (3432) 564-619, 564-691, 629-888 Rwanda Kigali -[250] 505601/2/3, 72126, 77147

Samoa Apia -[685] 21-631, after hours Tel 23-617, Mobile Tel [685] 7-1776

Saudi Arabia Riyadh -[966] (1) 488-3800; Dhahran -[966] (3) 3303200; Jeddah -[966] (2) 667-0080 Senegal Dakar -[221] 823-4296 or 823-7384

Sierra Leone Freetown -[232] (22) 226-481 through 226-485

Singapore Singapore -[65] 476-9100

Slovakia Bratislava -[421] (2) 5443-3338, Consulate Tel 5443-3338

Slovenia Ljubljana -[01] 200-5000

South Africa Johannesburg -[27] (11) 644-8000; Cape Town -[27] (21) 421-4280 thru 90; Durban -[27] (31) 305-7600; Pretoria -[27] (12) 342-1048

South Korea Seoul -[82] (2) 397-4114

Spain Madrid -[34] 91587-2200; Barcelona -[34] (93) 280-2227; Fuengirola (Malaga) -[34]952-474-891; La Coruna -[34] 981-213-233; Las Palmas -[34] 928-271-259; Palma de Mallorca -[34] 971-725-051; Seville -[34] (95) 423-1885; Valencia -[34] 96-351-6973

Sri Lanka Colombo -[94] (1) 448007

Sudan Khartoum -[249] (11) 774700 or 774611

Suriname Paramaribo -[597] 472900, 477881, 476459

Swaziland Mbabane -[268] 404-6441/5

Sweden Stockholm -[46] (8) 783-5300, after hours Tel 783-5310

Switzerland Bern -[41] (31) 357-7011, After-hours 357-7218; Geneva -[41] (22) 840-5160; Zurich -[41] (01) 422-2566

Syria Damascus -[963] (11) 333-1342, after hours: 333-3232

Tajikistan Dushanbe -[7] (3272)58-79-61

Tanzania Dar Es Salaam -[255] (22) 2666010/1/2/3/4/5

Thailand Bangkok -[66] (2) 205-4000; Chiang Mai -[66] (53) 252-629

Togo Lome -[228] 2212991/4

Trinidad and Tobago Port-of-Spain -(868) 622-6372/6, 6176

Tunisia Tunis -[216] (1) 782-566

Turkey Ankara -[90] (312) 455-5555; Adana -[90] (322) 459-1551; Istanbul -[90] (212) 2513602; Izmir -[90] (232) 441-0072 and 441-2203

Turkmenistan Ashgabat -[9] (9312) 350045

Uganda Kampala -[256] (41) 259-792 Ukraine Kiev -[380] (44) 490-4000, after hours Tel 216-3805

United Arab Emirates Abu Dhabi -[971] (2) 443-6691 or 443-6692, after hours Tel 443-4457; Dubai -[971] (4) 311-6000

United Kingdom London, England -[44] (20) 7499-9000; Belfast, Northern Ireland -[44] (2890) 328239; Edinburgh, Scotland -[44] (131) 556-8315

Uruguay Montevideo -[598] (2) 203-60-61 or 418-77-77

Uzbekistan Tashkent -[998] (71) 120-5450 Vatican City Vatican City -[39] (06) 4674-3428

Venezuela Caracas -[58] (212) 975-6411/9821; Maracaibo -[58] (61) 982-164 or 925-953 Vietnam Hanoi -(84) (4) 772-1500; Ho Chi Minh City -[84] (8) 8229433

Yemen Sanaa -[967] (1) 303-155, 303-182, After Hours: 303-166

Yugoslavia Belgrade -[381] (11) 361-3944, after hours Tel 646-481

Zambia Lusaka -[260] (1) 250-955 or 252-230, after hours Tel 252-234

Zimbabwe Harare -263] (4) 250-593/4/5

Appendix B

KEY WORD S.U.R.V.I.V.A.L.

The keyword SURVIVAL is a military acronym used to help troops prioritize and organize themselves should they find themselves cut off from anyone who could help them and need to survive in the wilderness and orchestrate or facilitate rescue, either by helping themselves to be found or by navigating their way back to safety, living off the land until they do.

Use the keyword SURVIVAL as soon as you identify that you are in a real-world survival situation. Each letter in the word SURVIVAL stands for a different rule.

S—Size up the situation. Inventory your equipment. Consider who is with you, and your familiarity with the environment you are in.

U—Undue haste makes waste. You don't want to make hasty decisions in a survival situation. Hasty decisions are often careless ones and carelessness in a survival scenario can be deadly. Take it slow and think out every move you make out.

R—Remember where you are. One of your first priorities in a survival situation is to know your location on the ground. If you don't know where you are, it is extremely difficult to figure out where you are going. If you want to have any chance of moving to safety and facilitating your rescue, the worst thing you can do is to wander aimlessly through the wilderness.

V—Vanquish fear and panic. Fear is nature's way of telling you to stay alert and pay attention to your surroundings. Fear can be a good thing at healthy levels. It is when you allow fear to debilitate your actions that it becomes panic. Panic is the worst possible thing you can do in a survival scenario. The main reason people panic is fear of the unknown. The best way to combat and control your fear is to have the courage to face it and recognize it. Once you understand your fear, you will be able to better control it and not let it develop into panic.

I—Improvise. In a survival situation, you may have very few resources to use to help you to survive the situation that you are in. It is imperative that you look around you and use every tool and resource that you have at your disposal for as many different purposes as you can think of. Don't let anything go to waste.

V—Value living. Never give up! Facing a survival scenario may be the hardest thing you have ever done, as well as the most physically and mentally demanding situation you have ever found yourself in. If you don't value your own life enough to drive forward through adversity, then there is a real possibility that you will die before effecting self-recovery or being rescued.

A—Act like the natives. Look around you. No matter what environment you are in, there are native people, animals, and plants that are not only surviving but thriving. If you want to survive, pay attention to how they find food, water, and shelter, and how they adapt to their environments in order to survive.

L—Live by your wits (but for now, learn basic skills). As far as living by your wits, all humans have a "sixth sense," or a little voice inside of your head that alerts you to danger and lets you know when to keep your head on a swivel. The key is to learn to listen to that little voice instead of suppressing it like so many of us do. Learn basic survival skills. Trying to learn survival skills after you have found yourself in a survival scenario is not the way to go about doing things. You should read books, watch videos, take classes, and practice your bushcraft skills to the point where your survival instincts and knowledge base is ready to tackle any survival situation or scenario that life has to throw at you.

Photo Credit: GettyImages

Appendix C

HOW TO REMAIN SAFE DURING THUNDERSTORMS AND LIGHTNING

*The following guidance was provided by www.ready.gov, an outstanding website for emergency preparedness information.

Lightning is a leading cause of injury and death from weather-related hazards. Although most lightning victims survive, people struck by lightning often report a variety of long-term, debilitating symptoms. Thunderstorms are dangerous storms that include lightning and can:

- Include powerful winds over 50 mph
- Create hail
- Cause flash flooding and tornadoes

IF YOU ARE UNDER A THUNDERSTORM WARNING, FIND SAFE SHELTER RIGHT AWAY

- When thunder roars, go indoors
- Move from outdoors into a building or car
- Pay attention to alerts and warnings
- Unplug appliances
- Do not use landline phones

HOW TO STAY SAFE WHEN A THUNDERSTORM THREATENS

Prepare NOW

- Know your area's risk for thunderstorms. In most places, they can occur year-round and at any hour.
- Sign up for your community's warning system. The Emergency Alert System (EAS) and National Oceanic and Atmospheric Administration (NOAA) Weather Radio also provide emergency alerts.
- Identify nearby, sturdy buildings close to where you live, work, study, and play.
- Cut down or trim trees that may be in danger of falling on your home.
- Consider buying surge protectors, lightning rods, or a lightning protection system to protect your home, appliances, and electronic devices.

Survive DURING

- A sturdy building is the safest place to be during a thunderstorm.
- Pay attention to weather reports and warnings of thunderstorms. Be ready to change plans, if necessary, to be near shelter.
- When you receive a thunderstorm warning or hear thunder, go inside immediately.
- If indoors, avoid running water or using landline phones. Electricity can travel through plumbing and phone lines.
- Protect your property. Unplug appliances and other electric devices. Secure outside furniture.
- If boating or swimming, get to land and find a sturdy, grounded shelter or vehicle immediately.
- If necessary, take shelter in a car with a metal top and sides. Do not touch anything metal.
- Avoid flooded roadways. Turn around. Don't drown! Just six inches of fast-moving water can knock you down, and one foot of moving water can sweep your vehicle away.

Be Safe AFTER

- Listen to authorities and weather forecasts for information on whether it is safe to go outside and instructions regarding potential flash flooding.
- Watch for fallen power lines and trees. Report them immediately.

Appendix D

SAFETY TIPS FOR SNOWSTORMS AND EXTREME COLD

The following guidance was provided by www.ready.gov, an outstanding website for emergency preparedness information.

Winter storms create a higher risk of car accidents, hypothermia, frostbite, carbon monoxide poisoning, and heart attacks from overexertion. Winter storms and blizzards can bring extreme cold, freezing rain, snow, ice, and high winds. A winter storm can:

- Last a few hours or several days
- Knock out heat, power, and communication services
- Place older adults, young children, and sick individuals at greater risk

IF YOU ARE UNDER A WINTER STORM WARNING, FIND SHELTER RIGHT AWAY

- Stay off roads.
- Stay indoors and dress warmly.
- Prepare for power outages.
- Use generators outside only and keep them away from windows.
- Listen for emergency information and alerts.
- Look for signs of hypothermia and frostbite.
- Check on neighbors.

HOW TO STAY SAFE WHEN A WINTER STORM THREATENS

Prepare NOW

- Know your area's risk for winter storms. Extreme winter weather can leave communities without utilities or other services for long periods of time.
- Prepare your home to keep out the cold with insulation, caulking, and weather stripping. Learn how to keep pipes from freezing. Install and test smoke alarms and carbon monoxide detectors with battery backups.
- Pay attention to weather reports and warnings of freezing weather and winter storms. Sign up for your community's warning system. The Emergency Alert System (EAS) and National Oceanic and Atmospheric Administration (NOAA) Weather Radio also provide emergency alerts.
- Gather supplies in case you need to stay home for several days without power. Keep in mind each person's specific needs, including medication. Do not forget the needs of pets. Have extra batteries for radios and flashlights.
- Create an emergency supply kit for your car. Include jumper cables, sand, a flashlight, warm clothes, blankets, bottled water, and non-perishable snacks. Keep the gas tank full.
- Learn the signs of, and basic treatments for, frostbite and hypothermia.

Survive DURING

- Stay off roads if at all possible. If trapped in your car, then stay inside.
- Limit your time outside. If you need to go outside, wear layers of warm clothing. Watch for signs of frostbite and hypothermia.
- Avoid carbon monoxide poisoning. Only use generators and grills outdoors and away from windows. Never heat your home with a gas stovetop or oven.

- Reduce the risk of a heart attack. Avoid overexertion when shoveling snow.
- Watch for signs of frostbite and hypothermia and begin treatment right away.
- Check on neighbors. Older adults and young children are more at risk in extreme cold.

Recognize and Respond

- Frostbite causes loss of feeling and color around the face, fingers, and toes.
  - » Signs: Numbness, white or grayish-yellow skin, firm or waxy skin
  - » Actions: Go to a warm room. Soak in warm water. Use body heat to warm. Do not massage or use a heating pad.

Hypothermia is an unusually low body temperature. A temperature below 95°F is an emergency.

  - » Signs: Shivering, exhaustion, confusion, fumbling hands, memory loss, slurred speech, or drowsiness
  - » Actions: Go to a warm room. Warm the center of the body first—chest, neck, head, and groin. Keep dry and wrapped up in warm blankets, including the head and neck.

Photo Credit: GettyImages

Appendix E

CYBERSECURITY

The following guidance was provided by www.ready.gov, an out-standing website for emergency preparedness information.

Cybersecurity involves preventing, detecting, and responding to cyberattacks that can have wide-ranging effects on the individual, organizations, the community, and at the national level.

Cyberattacks are malicious attempts to access or damage a computer system. Cyberattacks can lead to loss of money, theft of personal information, and damage to your reputation and safety. They are malicious attempts to access or damage a computer system.

Cyberattacks:

- Can use computers, mobile phones, gaming systems, and other devices
- Can include identity theft
- Can block your access or delete your personal documents and pictures
- Can target children
- Can cause delays and shutdowns of business services, transportation, and power

PROTECT YOURSELF AGAINST A CYBERATTACK

- Keep software and operating systems up-to-date
- Use strong passwords and two-factor authentication (two methods of verification).

- Watch for suspicious activity. When in doubt, don't click. Do not provide personal information.
- Use encrypted (secure) Internet communications.
- Create backup files.
- Protect your home and/or business Wi-Fi network.

Before a Cyberattack

You can increase your chances of avoiding cyber risks by setting up the proper controls. The following are things you can do to protect yourself, your family, and your property before a cyberattack occurs:

- Use strong passwords that are twelve characters or longer. Use upper and lowercase letters, numbers, and special characters. Change passwords monthly. Use a password manager.
- Use a stronger authentication such as a PIN or password that only you would know. Consider using a separate device that can receive a code or uses a biometric scan (e.g., fingerprint scanner).
- Watch for suspicious activity that asks you to do something right away, offers something that sounds too good to be true, or needs your personal information. Think before you click.
- Check your account statements and credit reports regularly.
- Use secure Internet communications.
- Use sites that use HTTPS if you will access or provide any personal information. Do not use sites with invalid certificates. Use a Virtual Private Network (VPN) that creates a secure connection.
- Use antivirus solutions, malware, and firewalls to block threats.
- Regularly back up your files in an encrypted file or encrypted file storage device.
- Limit the personal information you share online. Change privacy settings and do not use location features.
- Protect your home network by changing the administrative

and Wi-Fi passwords regularly. When configuring your router, choose the Wi-Fi Protected Access 2 (WPA2) Advanced Encryption Standard (AES) setting, which is the strongest encryption option.

During a Cyberattack

At Home

- Limit the damage. Look for unexplained charges, strange accounts on your credit report, unexpected denial of your credit card, posts you did not make showing up on your social networks, and people receiving emails you never sent.
- Immediately change passwords for all of your online accounts.
- Scan and clean your device.
- Consider turning off the device. Take it to a professional to scan and fix.
- Let work, school, or other system owners know.
- Contact banks, credit card companies, and other financial accounts. You may need to place holds on accounts that have been attacked. Close any unauthorized credit or charge accounts. Report that someone may be using your identity.
- Check to make sure the software on all of your systems is up to date.
- Run a scan to make sure your system is not infected or acting suspiciously.
- If you find a problem, disconnect your device from the Internet and perform a full system restore.
- If in a public setting, immediately inform a librarian, teacher, or manager in charge to contact their IT department.

After a Cyberattack

- File a report with the Office of the Inspector General (OIG) if you think someone is illegally using your Social Security number. OIG reviews cases of waste, fraud, and abuse. To file a report, visit **www.idtheft.gov.**

- You can also call the Social Security Administration hotline at 1-800-269-0271. For additional resources and more information, visit **http://oig.ssa.gov/report.**
- File a complaint with the FBI Internet Crime Complaint Center (IC3) at www.IC3.gov. They will review the complaint and refer it to the appropriate agency.
- Learn tips, tools, and more at **www.dhs.gov/stopthinkconnect.**
- File a report with the local police so there is an official record of the incident.
- Report identity theft to the **Federal Trade Commission.**
- Contact additional agencies depending on what information was stolen. Examples include contacting the Social Security Administration if your social security number was compromised, or the Department of Motor Vehicles if your driver's license or car registration has been stolen.
- Report online crime or fraud to your local United States Secret Service (USSS) **Electronic Crimes Task Force or the Internet Crime Complaint Center.**
- For further information on preventing and identifying threats, visit US-CERT's **Alerts and Tips page.**

Appendix F

HOW TO SURVIVE A PANDEMIC

Photo Credit: GettyImages

The following guidance was provided by www.ready.gov, an outstanding website for emergency preparedness information.

BEFORE A PANDEMIC
- Store a two-week supply of water and food.
- Periodically check your regular prescription drugs to ensure a continuous supply in your home.
- Have any nonprescription drugs and other health supplies on hand, including pain relievers, stomach remedies, cough and cold medicines, fluids with electrolytes, and vitamins.

- Get copies and maintain electronic versions of health records from doctors, hospitals, pharmacies, and other sources and store them, for personal reference. Get help accessing electronic help records.
- Talk with family members and loved ones about how they would be cared for if they got sick, or what will be needed to care for them in your home.

DURING A PANDEMIC
Limit the Spread of Germs and Prevent Infection

- **Avoid close contact** with people who are sick.
- When you are sick, **keep your distance** from others to protect them from getting sick too.
- **Cover your mouth and nose** with a tissue when coughing or sneezing. It may prevent those around you from getting sick.
- **Washing your hands** often will help protect you from germs.
- **Avoid touching your eyes, nose, or mouth.**
- **Practice other good health habits.** Get plenty of sleep, be physically active, manage your stress, drink plenty of fluids, and eat nutritious food.

Appendix G

PET PREPAREDNESS

The following guidance was provided by www.ready.gov, an outstanding website for emergency preparedness information.

WHAT YOU SHOULD KNOW ABOUT PET PREPAREDNESS

- Include your pets in your emergency plans.
- Build a separate emergency kit for your pets.
- Make sure to keep digital records and/or pictures to identify your pet after a disaster in case you become separated.
- Create a list of places that accept pets if an emergency happens.

GRAPHICS, HASHTAGS, VIDEOS, AND RELATED LINKS

- #PetPreparedness
- Pet preparedness graphics
- Download the FEMA app for disaster resources, weather alerts, and safety tips.
- "Preparing Makes Sense for Pet Owners" (4:22) on YouTube and the FEMA media library video
- The Humane Society of the United States
- American Society for the Prevention of Cruelty Towards Animals (ASPCA)
- Health and Human Services: Disaster Veterinary Technical Resources and Issues

GENERAL

- June is National #PetPreparedness Month. Include your pets in your family emergency plan: www.ready.gov/pets #PetPreparedness
- Preparing Makes Sense for Pet Owners. Watch this video for tips: https://www.youtube.com/watch?v=aUbSF_S20bE #PetPreparedness
- Don't forget to include your pets in your family's emergency plans. Share this one-minute video: https://youtu.be/BosQtZFv6Jk #PetPreparedness
- Download, share, or print @Readygov's Pet owner's planning guide with your community: http://www.fema.gov/media-library/assets/documents/90356 #PetPreparedness
- Don't forget to make a plan for large animals and livestock before a disaster. Tips: www.ready.gov/animals #Pet Preparedness
- Your pets can't make their own plans for #SevereWx but you can. Learn how to plan ahead at www.ready.gov/pets
- Are you traveling with your pets over the holidays? Pack a few emergency items for them too. www.ready.gov/pets #PetPreparedness

EMERGENCY KIT

- Take time to refresh your pet's emergency kit: Check water, food, and make sure their favorite toy is included to reduce stress www.ready.gov/pets
- Pets need an emergency supply kit too. View what items should go in it: www.ready.gov/pets #PetPreparedness
- A pet supply kit should contain the basics for survival, like pet food and water. #PetPreparedness
- Put a favorite toy, treats, or bedding in your pet's emergency kit to help reduce their stress. #PetPreparedness
- Add extra pet food and water to your grocery list to update your pet's emergency kit. #PetPreparedness
- Food, water, collar, and veterinary records are some items for your pet's emergency kit. More at: www.ready.gov/animals #PetPreparedness
- Take care of farm friends in an emergency. Pack emergency items for them too, including vehicles and trailers. #PetPreparedness
- Keep your pets' vet's name and vaccination records handy in case of emergency. #PetPreparedness
- Don't forget a pooper scooper, cat litter, or plastic bags in your pets' emergency kit! #PetPreparedness

EVACUATION

- Practice evacuating in the car with your animals, so they're more comfortable if you need to evacuate in an emergency. #PetPreparedness
- If officials tell you to evacuate before a storm, don't leave pets behind! https://www.ready.gov/animals #PetPreparedness
- Get your pet familiar with their carrier before #severewx hits, in case you need to evacuate with them quickly. #PetPreparedness
- Animals left behind in a disaster can easily be lost or injured—always take them with you if evacuate. #PetPreparedness

- If you evacuate your home, take your pets and their supplies with you. www.ready.gov/pets #PetPreparedness

SHELTER

- Make a list and check it twice. List the addresses and numbers of all the places you can take your pet in an emergency. #PetPreparedness
- Find out in advance where you can take your pets when an emergency happens in your community. https://www.gopetfriendly.com/ #PetPreparedness
- Identify pet shelters now before the next emergency: https://www.ready.gov/animals #PetPreparedness
- Pets displaced by a disaster are frequently kept in shelters or held by local orgs. Find a contact ahead of time. #PetPreparedness

IDENTIFICATION

- Keep that cute selfie of you and your pet in your emergency kit to prove ownership. #PetPreparedness
- Does your pet have ID? Put your name and contact information on your pet's ID tag in case you're separated in an emergency. #PetPreparedness
- A picture is worth a thousand words. Take a current photo of your pet in case you get separated during a disaster. #PetPreparedness
- Tip: Include the number of an out-of-town relative on your pet's ID tag. #PetPreparedness
- Think about microchipping your pet. These permanent implants help locate your pet following a disaster. #PetPreparedness
- Tip: Keep your pets' microchip registration info current so you can be contacted if your pets gets lost in a disaster. #PetPreparedness
- After a disaster, don't allow your pets to roam loose. Landmarks may have been changed and your pet could become disoriented. #PetPreparedness

SEASONAL

Keeping Animals Safe When It's Hot

- Never leave pets in the car! Temperatures rise quickly even with the windows down and can be deadly for your pet. #HeatSafety
- #BeatTheHeat indoors, check on neighbors and always call 911 if you see a pet or child in a hot car.
- Be sure your pets have access to plenty of water, especially when it's hot. #PetPreparedness #HeatSafety #BeattheHeat
- Make sure your pet has plenty of shady places to go when outdoors. #PetPreparedness #HeatSafety #BeattheHeat
- *Caution*: Test sidewalks with your hand. If it's too hot for your hand, it's probably too hot for your pet. #PetPreparedness #HeatSafety
- Avoid exercising with your pet outside on extremely hot days #PetPreparedness #HeatSafety

Keeping Animals Safe When It's Cold

- When you're cold, your pets are cold. Bring pets inside during cold weather! #WinterSafety
- Always bring your pets inside when it's freezing outside. #WinterSafety
- When the temperature drops, remember to bring your pets inside. If you see animals outside, call your local Humane Society or 311 if available.
- Don't forget to wipe your dog's paws! Ice-melting chemicals can make your pet sick. #PetPreparedness
- Your pet may think antifreeze is sweet, but it's not a dessert! Keep your pet safe this winter: http://bit.ly/1vKcaws #PetPreparedness
- Bring your furry friends inside when temperatures take a dip. #PetPreparedness
- #ColdWeather Tip: Bring your furry friends inside. Move

livestock to sheltered areas with non-frozen drinking water. #PetPreparedness

- Make sure pets are inside and out of the #snow. If you see pets wandering outside, call your local animal control agency. #PetPreparedness

About the Author

Brian Morris is a retired US Army Special Forces Master Sergeant. Serving on active duty for more than twenty-five years, he spent the majority of his time in service with the Special Forces as a Green Beret. He is a decorated combat veteran who served multiple tours in Afghanistan during the global war on terrorism since September 11, 2001. Brian has been deployed all over Africa, Bosnia, Iraq, Kuwait, Korea, Lebanon, and Saudi Arabia. Brian also taught at the

Survival, Evasion, Resistance, and Escape (SERE) School and wrote SERE doctrine for the Army Special Forces, including the Army Special Operations Forces Resistance and Escape Manual and the US Army Special Forces Personnel Recovery Manual. Additionally, he is an expert and master briefer in anti-terrorism and personal security techniques tactics and procedures. Mr. Morris holds a Bachelor of Arts degree in homeland security from the American Military University. After retiring from the Army in 2012, he spent a year in Afghanistan working as counterinsurgency advisor to the International Security and Assistance Force (ISAF) commander. After returning to the United States in 2013, Brian spent several years working as the chief personnel recovery advisor for the US Army Special Operations Command. During this time he wrote his first book on terrorism awareness, called the *Green Beret Pocket Guide,* which was published in 2014. After being diagnosed with leukemia in 2015, he took two years to fight his way into remission and by 2016 he was back to writing, with his second book, *SpecOps Shooting* published in 2016. He also took on a monthly writing commitment to *American Survival Guide* magazine, to whom he still contributes today. In 2018 Brian's third book, *SpecOps Bushcrafting,* was published. Today, Brian continues to write, works as a personal security consultant for high-risk travel, and runs a wilderness survival school. He is married and the father of three grown children. He lives on a small farm in central North Carolina with his wife and their dogs.